DESSERTS

Cakes and Tortes · Tarts · Pies · Pastries · Fruit Desserts · Ice Creams · Biscuits and Sweets · Tarts · Pies · Chocolates · Pastries · Cakes and Tortes · Fruit Desserts · Ice Creams · Biscuits and Sweets · Pies · Pastries

DESSERTS

THE COMPLETE GUIDE TO CREATING MORE THAN 80 CAKES, PIES, PASTRIES, AND MORE

ELIZABETH WOLF-COHEN

APPLE

A QUINTET BOOK

Published by the Apple Press
6 Blundell Street
London N7 9BH

ISBN 1-85076-795-5

This book was designed and produced by
Quintet Publishing Limited
6 Blundell Street
London N7 9BH

Creative Director: Richard Dewing
Art Director: Clare Reynolds
Designer: Ian Hunt
Project Editor: Kathy Steer
Editor: Anna Bennett
Illustrator: Joanne Makin

Typeset in Great Britain by
Central Southern Typesetters, Eastbourne
Manufactured in England by
D.P. Graphics, Holt, Wiltshire
Printed in Singapore by
Star Standard Industries (Pte) Ltd.

Contents

INTRODUCTION

I love desserts – I always have. As a child, desserts were only for special occasions and holidays. There was the occasional gingerbread cake or chocolate pudding, but on the whole after dinner there was fresh fruit. Maybe that explains my great passion for desserts.

Even now I get excited when I think of which dessert I should make when friends come round for dinner; somehow I always design the menu backwards – starting with the dessert and then deciding what the main course will be. When I eat out, I always read the dessert menu first to be sure I reserve something special, or order a soufflé or other dessert which has a twenty-minute wait or just make sure I leave enough room for some extraordinarily rich confection. Dessert for me is a real pleasure. It turns a simple dinner or occasion into something special. I simply cannot resist it.

Desserts is a compilation of desserts to die for – each one more tempting than the next. Some may be as simple as the Bittersweet Chocolate Soufflés or the classic Crème Caramel, others may be spectacular party pieces like the Celebration Brownie-Baked Alaska, but they are all heavenly. Each one is especially scrumptious in its way, even if simple in concept. A slice of Prune Coffee Cake with a foaming hot cappuccino on a wintry morning seems the ultimate pleasure at the time, while a bowl of cool, refreshing Tropical Fruit Salad with Thai-Scented Coconut Cream is just perfect on a hot, sultry night after a spicy barbecued meal.

Whatever the occasion, you'll find the perfect dessert in this collection. I have tried to include all the necessary techniques specific to different kinds of desserts, such as making perfect pastry, cooking custard without curdling and even successfully melting chocolate. Many recipes include tips for preparing ahead and ideas for decorating. Most of the equipment and ingredients required are found in the average kitchen or are available in cookware shops and supermarkets. Specialist items are explained and tips for finding them are given. Do make an effort to use the best quality ingredients you can afford, as the end result will be well worth it.

Whatever the occasion, or even if there is no occasion, a dessert shows family and friends you really care. Make one tonight and enjoy it.

CAKE MAKING

Cakes are among the world's favourite desserts. Many cakes have a long-standing tradition and often play a central role in celebrating special occasions from birthdays to weddings to christenings and many holidays as well. A perfect cake depends on good ingredients, the right utensils, careful measuring and accurate temperatures and timing.

There are many methods of making cakes, but whatever preparation is used, make sure all ingredients are at room temperature unless otherwise instructed. Eggs should not be cold, as a temperature contrast can curdle a creamed butter-sugar mixture.

The type of baking tin will affect the baking time, as well as the finish of the cake. Dark metal tins reduce the cooking time slightly and encourage a darker crust; loose-bottomed tins help in turning out fragile or delicate cakes and tortes, springform tins are essential for cheesecakes and heavy-based high-sided tins prevent rich fruit cakes from scorching on the bottom. It is important to use the correct tin: always use the type specified in a recipe.

PREHEATING AND TESTING

Be sure to preheat your oven at least 15 minutes before baking and, if necessary, use an oven thermometer to verify the temperature. Most cakes should be baked on the centre or bottom third shelf. If baking two or three layers, stagger the tins so they are not directly above each other and rotate them from front to back and top to bottom when the filling is adequately set.

There are several ways of testing cakes. A skewer is best for plain cakes which need to be baked through. Inserted into the centre, it should come out clean with no crumbs attached. Alternatively, press a fingertip lightly onto the center of the cake: it should spring back if done. Most cakes should bake to a golden brown and tend to shrink slightly from the side of the tin.

Many cakes can be stored for two to three days, wrapped well in an airtight tin. For longer periods, refrigerate or freeze until needed.

PASTRY MAKING

Pastry is one of the great foundations of dessert making and by following a few basic rules everyone can make good pastry.

There are three basic pastries: pie crust – a shortcrust flaky pastry which can vary in thickness; *pâté feuilletée* or puff pastry, the basis of napoleons and other French pastries, and cream puff or *choux* pastry, used for cream puffs and profiteroles.

Pastry can be made by hand or in a food processor. If using a machine remember to not overwork the dough; always stop before it forms a ball or the pastry will be tough. "Resting the dough" is essential for all pastry as is chilling the dough. Chilling helps the resting process and sets the fat, allowing for easier handling and less shrinkage.

The ingredients for pastry should be weighed as this produces more accurate results if you prefer not to make your own pastry, or are in a hurry, good-quality pastry is widely available in supermarkets. They give reliable results and make good standbys in your freezer.

LINING A TART TIN

The traditional tart tin is shallow with no rim. It has a fluted side and sometimes a removable bottom. This gives the characteristic edge and allows the side of the tin to be removed without disturbing the base. Flan rings are generally smooth-sided rings which are set on a heavy pastry sheet to form the base. The best tins are dull metal or nonstick, as shiny metal reflects the heat and prevents the crust from browning. Butter-rich dough does not generally stick, but I like to spray the tin lightly with a vegetable cooking spray. Alternatively, brush with a little oil.

1. To transfer rolled-out dough to a tart tin or pie dish, set the rolling pin on the near edge of the pastry round, square or rectangle. Fold the edge of the pastry over the rolling pin, then continue to roll dough loosely around pin.

2. Hold far edge of dough and rolling pin over far edge of the tin and gently unroll the dough, allowing it to settle in the tin without stretching or pulling. Using floured fingertips, lift outside edge of dough and ease into bottom and sides of tin, allowing excess pastry to overhang the edge.

3. To line a tart tin, smooth pastry on to the bottom of tin and press the overhang down slightly toward the centre of the tin, making the top edge thicker. Roll the rolling pin over the edge, cutting off any excess dough and flattening the top edge. Press the thickened top edge against the side of the tin to form a stand-up edge. This makes the edge slightly thicker and higher, reinforcing the sides of the pastry case. Prick the bottom and crimp or decorate the edge. Refrigerate 1 hour or freeze for 20 minutes.

LINING TARTLET TINS

A patty tin can be used for small tarts, or individual tartlet tins. For very small tartlet tins (less than 5 cm/ 2 inches): Arrange the tins on the work surface close together and unroll the rolled-out pastry over them, loosely draping the dough into them. Roll the rolling pin over them to cut off the excess pastry then, using a floured thumb, press the pastry on to the bottom and up the sides of the tins. Prick bottoms with a fork. For larger tartlets, I prefer to follow the steps for lining a round tart tin, as this ensures adequate pastry and a firm high edge to support any filling.

BAKING BLIND

Baking blind is a method of pre-baking a pastry case, either partially or completely, to prevent the pastry from becoming soggy and to ensure that the base cooks evenly and completely. Complete baking is necessary for an uncooked filling and partial baking blind is recommended when a liquid, creamy or custard-based filling is cooked completely in the pastry shell. The dough is generally weighted with dried beans, rice or pastry weights to prevent the pastry from shrinking and puffing too much.

1. Cut out a circle of baking paper or foil about three inches larger than the tart tin. Fold in half and lay it across the centre of the dough-lined tart tin. Unfold it and press on to the bottom, into the edge and up the sides of the dough.

2. Fill the lined tart shell with dried beans, rice or pastry weights and spread them evenly over the bottom and up the sides. The dried beans, rice or pastry weights can be cooled and saved to be reused.

3. To partially bake pastry blind: Bake in a 200°C/400°F/Gas Mark 6 oven 15–20 minutes until pastry is set and rim looks dry and slightly golden. Remove to a heatproof surface and remove paper or foil and beans. The shell can be filled and baking finished.

4. To completely bake pastry blind: Bake in a 200°C/400°F/Gas Mark 6 oven 20 minutes. Remove to a heatproof surface and remove paper or foil and beans. Prick the pastry bottom again and bake 10 minutes or until golden. The bottom should look dry and set. Cool before filling as recipe directs.

FRUIT DESSERTS

Fresh fruit forms the basis of many delicious desserts. In general, choose firm, yet ripe fruit for the best flavour. Fruit can be used fresh, cut-up, poached or puréed and in many other ways.

If using fresh fruit, sprinkle apples, pears, bananas, peaches and nectarines with a little lemon juice to prevent them from darkening. A swivel-bladed vegetable peeler is the best choice for peeling and can be used to core apples and pears as well. Avoid washing delicate berries if possible, as they absorb water and lose their flavour. Scrub oranges, lemons and limes if using the grated rind or for julienne strips; better still, look for untreated and unwaxed fruits.

Poached fruits can be served on their own or used as a part of a more elaborate dessert. Always prepare the poaching syrup first, adding the flavourings as the recipe directs, and dissolving the sugar completely before adding the fruit. Adjust the heat so the syrup barely simmers, then cover the fruit with a piece of baking or greaseproof paper. This helps to keep the fruit from floating and helps keep it immersed in the liquid. The cooking time will depend on the ripeness of the fruit; test by piercing the fruit with the blade of a sharp knife.

Puréed soft fruits make ideal sauces for desserts or can form the basis of other desserts. *Coulis* is a French word meaning a pourable purée and it is one of the easiest dessert sauces to make. Put 450 g/1 lb of fresh strawberries, raspberries, blackberries or mango or peach slices in a food processor fitted with a metal blade and process until smooth. Add sugar to taste and a little lemon juice, if you like, and process again. Press through a sieve and add a little liqueur, thinning with a little water if necessary.

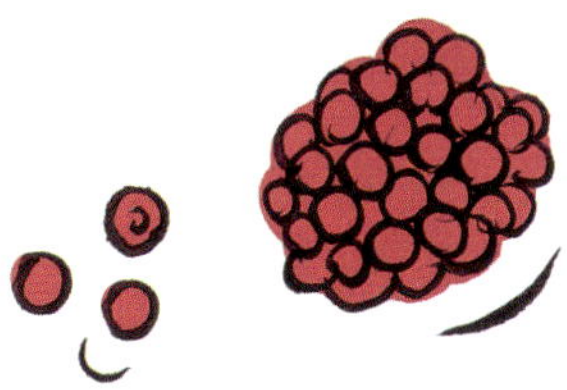

FROZEN DESSERTS

Frozen desserts are an ideal choice for parties and occasions of all kinds, as the dessert can be made well ahead and even decorated, then stored in the freezer until you are almost ready to serve.

Homemade ice-creams and sorbets can be served on their own or with a sauce or can be part of another dessert, like an ice-cream pie or a Baked Alaska. If you enjoy making ice-creams and frozen desserts, an electric ice-cream maker is a worthwhile investment.

If you don't have an ice-cream maker, pour the mixture into a freezerproof container and freeze for 2 hours until it begins to freeze around the edges. Remove the box from the freezer and whisk until the mixture is blended. Repeat for several hours until the mixture is frozen and smooth.

If adding any solids to the ice-cream, such as chocolate chips, raisins, nuts or even a fruit or chocolate swirl, do so after the mixture has frozen, as these solid pieces will clog an ice-cream machine or a swirl will become too well blended. Be sure to freeze the ice-cream mixture in a pretty bowl or glass dish if you plan to serve it at the table; otherwise a plastic freezer box with a tight-fitting lid will suffice.

To serve frozen desserts, allow to soften at room temperature for 15 minutes before serving, or 20–25 minutes in the refrigerator. For easier slicing, dip a thin-bladed knife into hot water before cutting (or an ice-cream scoop for scooping) each slice; wipe off excess water.

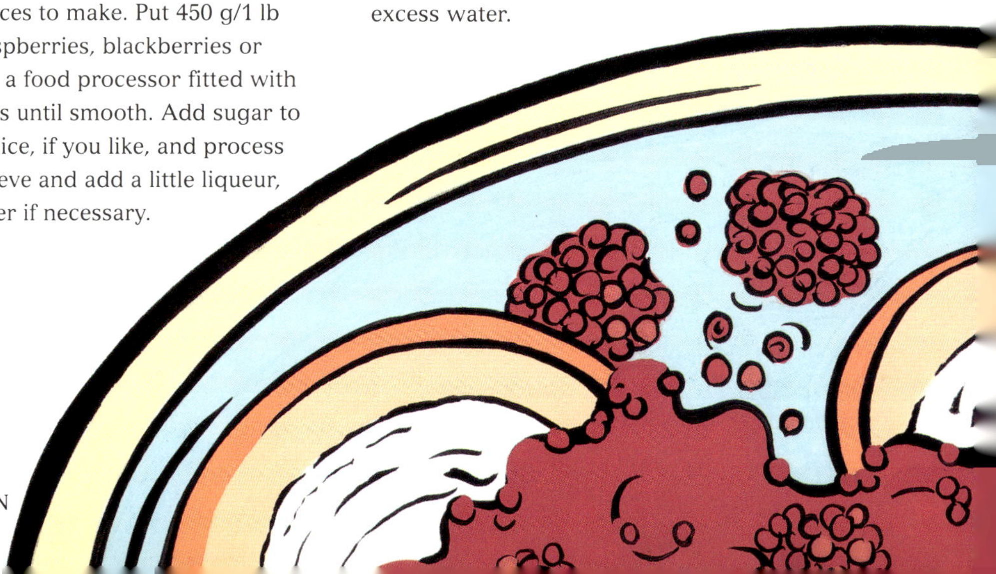

CUSTARDS, MOUSSES AND SOUFFLES

Many popular desserts are based on a custard – a mixture of milk, eggs and sugar, which is cooked over a low heat until thickened or baked in the oven in a bain-marie to form a dessert on its own, like Crème Caramel or Crème Brûlée.

The most important factor in cooking custard is heat. If the custard mixture becomes too hot, or heats too quickly, the custard will curdle and separate. Cook custard over low heat in a heavy-based saucepan or use a double boiler or heatproof bowl set over hot water. Beat the egg yolks and sugar until foamy and light, then pour the hot milk over the yolks, whisking constantly. This allows the milk to heat the egg mixture and start the cooking process. Return the mixture to the saucepan and stir constantly over low heat until the mixture thickens and coats the back of a spoon. If the custard does begin to curdle, remove from the heat and whisk in an ice cube to lower the temperature, or strain into a cold bowl or saucepan.

Baked custards need to cook gently in a bain-marie or water bath, which insulates them from direct heat and helps prevent curdling. Setting the dessert on a folded dish towel provides more insulation for very delicate mixtures. To test a set custard, shake the pan; the centre of the custard should wobble slightly, and a knife inserted halfway between the centre and the edge should come out clean.

Mousses and soufflés generally use beaten egg whites to provide a light, airy texture. Often the egg yolks are beaten until thick and mousse-like to provide a base, then beaten egg whites are folded in. Put the egg whites in a large, grease-free bowl, preferably copper or stainless steel, and with an electric mixer or whisk, beat until foamy or "broken". If not using a copper bowl, add a pinch of cream of tartar or salt, which helps the whites to stiffen, and continue beating on a higher speed until the whites hold soft peaks when the beaters or whisk are lifted from the bowl.

For meringue, add about three-quarters of the measured amount of sugar, a tablespoon at a time, beating well after each addition until the sugar is dissolved (test by rubbing a little meringue between thumb and finger – if it feels gritty, continue beating). Continue beating until stiff and glossy. Sprinkle over the last quarter of the measured sugar all at once and gently fold in.

Folding is a method of combining a light mixture with a heavier one without deflating the lighter mixture. Do not overbeat the egg whites. Begin by stirring a spoonful of the beaten whites into the heavier mixture to lighten it, as this will allow the remaining whites to be incorporated more easily. Spoon over the remaining whites and fold in by cutting down into the centre of the mixture to the bottom of the bowl, turning the mixture over itself with a rolling motion. Continue until the whites are just blended in but don't overwork the mixture or the whites will deflate.

If the whites are well beaten and stable, a mousse will have a firm yet light texture and will be able to support its own weight, and a soufflé will rise high in the oven to make a soft, light and airy dessert.

Remember to butter the soufflé dish right up to the edge as it is the butter which helps lead the soufflé up the sides of the dish. To serve, "crack" the top open with a spoon and serve each guest some of the firm top with some of the softer centre – the ideal combination of textures.

CHAPTER ONE

CAKES and TORTES

Lime Coconut Layer Cake
with Seven-Minute Icing

8–10 SERVINGS

Delicious layers of lime-scented sponge with a tangy lime custard topped with classic seven-minute icing and coconut – a desert island dream dessert.

CAKE

100 g/4 oz plain flour
Pinch of salt
6 eggs
175 g/6 oz caster sugar
Grated rind of 2 limes
1 tsp lime juice
75 g/3 oz desiccated coconut

LIME CUSTARD

2 Tbsp cornflour
250 ml/8 fl oz cold water
2 eggs
Grated rind and juice of 1 large lime
225 g/8 oz granulated sugar
75 g/3 oz butter

SEVEN-MINUTE ICING

2 egg whites
350 g/12 oz granulated sugar
3 Tbsp cold water
1/4 tsp cream of tartar
1 1/2 tsp golden syrup
1 1/2 Tbsp lime juice
75 g/3 oz desiccated coconut

1. Preheat oven to 180°C/350°F/Gas Mark 4. Lightly grease three 20 cm/8 inch cake tins. Line the bottom of each with nonstick baking paper; regrease and flour tins. Sift the flour and salt.

2. Put the eggs in a large heatproof bowl and set over a saucepan of just simmering water. With an electric mixer, beat until frothy. Gradually beat in the sugar until well blended. Continue beating until the mixture is doubled in volume and very thick.

3. Remove the bowl from the pan of water and fold in the grated lime rind, juice and desiccated coconut. Sift in the flour mixture in three batches, folding in after each addition.

4. Divide the mixture evenly among the tins. Bake about 30 minutes. Cool for 5 minutes. Turn out on to a wire rack to cool completely.

5. Prepare the lime custard: Blend the cornflour with about a tablespoon of the cold water to dissolve. Whisk in the remaining eggs. Put the remaining water, grated rind and lime juice, sugar and butter in a saucepan and, over medium heat, bring to a boil. Whisk a little of the mixture into the beaten egg mixture, then whisk the egg mixture into the saucepan and return to the heat. Whisk until the mixture boils, about 5 minutes. Pour into a bowl and cool.

6. Prepare the icing: Put all the ingredients except the coconut in a heatproof mixing bowl and set over a saucepan of just simmering water. With an electric mixer, beat for 7 minutes until thick. Remove from the hot water and beat until the mixture is at room temperature. Cover with cling film.

7. Remove the paper from the cake layers. Place a layer on a plate and spread with half the lime custard. Cover with a second layer and the remaining lime custard. Spread the top and side of the cake with the icing and press some of the desiccated coconut on to the side of the cake; sprinkle the remaining coconut over the top.

White Chocolate Mousse and Strawberry Layer Cake

10 SERVINGS

Other fresh berries in season can be used in this cake, but strawberries look particularly elegant.

100 g/4 oz good-quality white chocolate, grated
120 ml/4 fl oz double cream
120 ml/4 fl oz milk
1 Tbsp rum or vanilla essence
225 g/8 oz plain flour
1 tsp baking powder
Pinch of salt
100 g/4 oz unsalted butter, softened
175 g/6 oz caster sugar
3 eggs
675 g/1½ lb fresh strawberries, sliced, plus extra for decoration
350 ml/12 fl oz double cream
2 Tbsp rum or strawberry-flavoured liqueur
1 Tbsp icing sugar, sifted

WHITE CHOCOLATE MOUSSE FILLING

300 g/10 oz good-quality white chocolate, chopped
350 ml/12 fl oz double cream
2 Tbsp rum or strawberry-flavoured liqueur

1. Preheat oven to 180°C/350°F/Gas Mark 4. Lightly butter two deep 22 cm/9 inch cake tins. Line bottoms with nonstick baking paper; regrease and flour tins. Put the white chocolate and cream in a saucepan and stir over low heat until melted and smooth. Stir in the milk and rum or vanilla essence. Cool.

2. Sift together the flour, baking powder and salt. Set aside. With an electric mixer, beat the butter and sugar until light and creamy. Add the eggs, one at a time, beating well after each addition.

3. Add the flour mixture alternately with the melted chocolate mixture in three batches until just blended. Scrape into the prepared tins and bake 20–25 minutes or until done. Cool in tins 10 minutes. Turn out on to a wire rack to cool completely.

4. Prepare the mousse: Process the chopped white chocolate in a food processor 15–30 seconds. Bring the cream to a boil. Pour the hot cream through the processor feed tube and process until smooth. Pour into a bowl, stir in the rum or strawberry-flavoured liqueur and refrigerate until just set. Whisk until light and mousse-like.

5. To assemble: Remove the paper from the cake bottoms. Slice each cake into two layers. Place one layer, cut-side up, on a cake plate and spread with one-third of the mousse mixture. Arrange one-third of the sliced strawberries over the mousse. Place a second layer on top and continue layering in this way. Cover with the last cake layer.

6. Whip the cream with the rum or liqueur and icing sugar until firm peaks form. Spread half over top and sides of cake. Pipe scrolls or rosettes with remaining cream around top edge of cake and in the centre. Decorate with remaining strawberries.

Jewish Apple Cake

10–12 SERVINGS

Apple cakes are traditionally popular in the Jewish community. This one is made with oil, keeping it moist and giving it a rich texture.

APPLE FILLING

900 g/2 lb cooking apples, peeled, cored and thinly sliced
4 Tbsp sugar
1 tsp cinnamon
Grated rind and juice of 1 lemon

CAKE

4 eggs
300 g/10 oz caster sugar
275 ml/9 fl oz vegetable oil
200 g/7 oz plain flour
2 tsp baking powder
1½ tsp vanilla essence
3 to 4 Tbsp granulated sugar for sprinkling

1. Preheat oven to 180°C/350°F/Gas Mark 4. Grease and lightly flour a 22 x 32 cm/9 x 13 inch cake tin, preferably nonstick. Toss the apple slices with sugar, cinnamon, lemon rind and juice.

2. With an electric mixer, beat the eggs with the sugar until thick and pale and the mixture leaves a ribbon trail, 7 minutes. Gradually beat in the oil until blended. Fold in flour, baking powder and vanilla.

3. Pour half the batter into the tin, spreading evenly. Spoon half the apple mixture over the batter. Cover the apple mixture with the remaining batter and top with the remaining apple mixture, spreading it into an even layer. Sprinkle generously with sugar.

4. Bake until cake is golden and puffy, the apples are tender and the centre springs back when pressed gently with a fingertip, 1¼–1½ hours. Cover with foil if the top browns too quickly. Remove to a wire rack and cool 30 minutes in the tin. Serve warm.

Devil's Food Dream Cake

10–12 SERVINGS

These rich, dark chocolate layers are filled and iced with a dark chocolate ganache, a chocolate truffle icing. Truly the work of a devil's dream.

25 g/1 oz cocoa powder
250 g/9 oz extra fine flour
2 tsp bicarbonate of soda
1/2 tsp salt
50 g/2 oz unsweetened chocolate, chopped
100 g/4 oz unsalted butter, softened
450 g/1 lb soft brown sugar
2 tsp vanilla essence
3 eggs
175 ml/6 fl oz soured cream
1 tsp vinegar
250 ml/8 fl oz boiling water

CHOCOLATE GANACHE ICING

450 ml/3/4 pt double cream
675 g/1 1/2 lb good-quality bittersweet or plain chocolate, chopped
25 g/1 oz butter
1 Tbsp vanilla essence

1. Preheat oven to 190°C/375°F/Gas Mark 5. Grease two 22 cm/9 inch cake tins. Line bottoms with nonstick baking paper; regrease and flour tins. Sift together the cocoa powder, flour, bicarbonate of soda and salt; set aside.

2. In the top of a double-boiler over low heat, melt the chocolate, stirring frequently until smooth. Cool.

3. With an electric mixer, beat the butter, brown sugar and vanilla until light and creamy. Add the eggs, one at a time, beating well after each addition.

4. Add the flour mixture alternately with the soured cream in three batches. Stir in the vinegar and slowly beat in the boiling water. Pour into the tins and bake 20–25 minutes. Cool the cakes in their tins 5 minutes. Carefully turn out on to a wire rack to cool.

5. Prepare the icing: Bring the cream to the boil. Remove from heat and add the chocolate all at once, stirring until melted. Beat in the butter and vanilla. Pour into a bowl and refrigerate until the ganache reaches a spreading consistency.

6. To assemble: Remove paper from cake bottoms. Slice each cake into two layers. Place one layer, cut side up on a plate and spread with one-sixth of ganache. Place second layer on top and ice with another sixth of ganache. Continue layering. Ice the top and sides of cake with remaining ganache.

Chocolate Pecan Torte

12–16 SERVINGS

A torte is a continental type of cake that generally uses ground nuts or breadcrumbs instead of flour to bind the eggs and butter. This torte is extremely rich and a little goes a long way.

150 g/5 oz pecan halves
100 g/4 oz caster sugar
200 g/7 oz good-quality plain or bittersweet chocolate, chopped
150 g/5 oz unsalted butter, cut into pieces
4 eggs
1 tsp rum or vanilla essence
1 tsp cinnamon
24 toasted pecan halves for decoration (optional)

CHOCOLATE-HONEY GLAZE

100 g/4 oz plain or bittersweet chocolate, chopped
50 g/2 oz unsalted butter, cut into pieces
2 Tbsp honey
1/2 tsp cinnamon

1. Preheat oven to 180°C/350°F/Gas Mark 4. Spread the pecans on a biscuit sheet and toast until lightly browned 3–5 minutes. When cool, process the pecans in a food processor with 1 tablespoon of the sugar for 30–45 seconds until fine crumbs form. (Do not overprocess.)

2. Butter a 20 cm/8 inch cake tin, line the bottom with nonstick baking paper and butter again. Melt the chocolate and butter until smooth, remove from the heat and cool slightly.

3. Beat the eggs with the remaining sugar and rum or vanilla essence until frothy. Beat in the melted chocolate, then stir in the ground pecans and cinnamon. Pour into the tin.

4. Place the cake tin into a roasting tin and pour in enough boiling water to come 2 cm/3/4 inch up the side of the cake tin. Bake 25–30 minutes until the edge of the torte is set, but the centre is slightly soft. Remove cake to a wire rack to cool.

5. Prepare the glaze: Heat the chocolate, butter, honey and cinnamon until melted, stirring constantly; remove from heat. Dip each pecan half halfway into the glaze, allow excess to drain off and place on a nonstick baking paper-lined biscuit sheet until set.

6. Loosen the torte from the side of the tin with a knife. Turn out on to a wire rack placed over a biscuit sheet. Remove the lining paper. Pour the glaze over the top of the torte and spread evenly. Allow to set slightly, then arrange the chocolate-dipped nuts around the outside edge of the torte and allow the glaze to set completely. Refrigerate at least 2 hours or overnight. Serve at room temperature.

Rich Lemon Pound Cake

8–10 SERVINGS

200 g/7 oz plain flour
2 tsp baking powder
1/4 tsp salt
225 g/8 oz unsalted butter, softened
225 g/8 oz caster sugar
4 eggs, lightly beaten
Grated rind of 1 lemon
1 tsp lemon essence
1/2 tsp vanilla essence

LEMON GLAZE

150 g/5 oz icing sugar, sifted
2 to 4 Tbsp lemon juice

1. Preheat oven to 170°C/325°F/Gas Mark 3. Grease and flour a 20 x 10 cm/8 x 4 inch loaf tin. Sift together the flour, baking powder and salt.

2. With an electric mixer, beat the butter at medium speed until soft. Gradually add the sugar and then beat until light and creamy, 5 minutes.

3. Add the beaten eggs a tablespoon at a time, beating well after each addition. If the mixture begins to curdle, sprinkle in a little of the flour mixture.

4. Add the flour mixture in three batches, folding in lightly with a spoon until just blended. Stir in the lemon rind, lemon essence and vanilla essence.

5. Scrape the batter gently into the tin, smoothing the top and making a slight indentation along the centre. Bake 30 minutes until golden and the centre springs back when pressed with a fingertip.

6. Remove to a wire rack and cool in the tin 10 minutes. Turn out on to the wire rack and turn top-side up to cool completely.

7. Sift the icing sugar into a small bowl and gradually stir in enough lemon juice until a smooth glaze is formed. Gently spoon over the warm cake and allow to set before slicing.

Prune Coffee Cake

10–12 SERVINGS

My Polish neighbours serve this cake with mid-morning coffee. The chocolate glaze makes this cake extra-special.

350 g/12 oz plain flour
1½ tsp bicarbonate of soda
1 tsp baking powder
225 g/8 oz unsalted butter, cut into pieces
Grated rind of 1 orange
450 g/1 lb caster sugar
1 Tbsp vanilla or rum essence
¼ tsp salt
75 ml/16 fl oz soured cream
3 eggs, lightly beaten
*75 g/3 oz prune purée**
50 g/2 oz chopped walnuts or pecans
2 Tbsp cocoa powder, sifted
1 tsp cinnamon

CHOCOLATE-HONEY GLAZE

75 g/3 oz plain or bittersweet chocolate, chopped
45 g/1½ oz unsalted butter
1½ Tbsp honey

1. Preheat oven to 180°C/350°F/Gas Mark 4. Grease and flour a heavy 25 cm/10 inch hollow ring tin (preferably nonstick). Sift the flour, bicarbonate of soda and baking powder.

2. Melt the butter in a saucepan. Stir in the orange rind and remove from heat. Immediately stir in the sugar, vanilla or rum essence, salt, soured cream and eggs, then beat in all the flour mixture until blended.

3. Spoon about half the batter into the tin. Stir the prune purée and drop heaped tablespoonfuls over the centre of the batter. Sprinkle the walnuts or pecans, cocoa powder and cinnamon over the top of the prune purée.

4. Spoon the remaining batter over the prune purée and nut mixture and smooth the top evenly. Draw a palette knife through the mixtures creating a swirling pattern. Bake 50 minutes. Cool in the pan 10 minutes.

5. Invert the cake on to a wire rack to cool completely. Melt the chocolate, butter and honey. Drizzle the glaze over the cake and allow to set.

*To make your own prune purée, simmer 175 g/6 oz prunes with 100 g/4 oz water, a little grated orange rind and about 2 tablespoons orange juice until all the liquid is absorbed and the prunes form a mushy purée. Blend in a food processor. Store, covered, in the refrigerator.

Blueberry Cream Cheese Streusel Cake

10–12 SERVINGS

This delicious cake is a cross between a blueberry muffin and a cheese Danish – perfect with cappuccino.

STREUSEL TOPPING

100 g/4 oz unsalted butter, softened
150 g/5 oz caster sugar
50 g/2 oz soft brown sugar
75 g/3 oz plain flour
50 g/2 oz chopped toasted almonds
1½ tsp cinnamon
½ tsp freshly ground nutmeg
¼ tsp salt

CREAM CHEESE FILLING

350 g/12 oz cream cheese
75 g/3 oz caster sugar
1 egg
1 Tbsp lemon juice
1 tsp almond essence

CAKE

450 g/1 lb plain flour
4 tsp baking powder
1 tsp salt
100 g/4 oz unsalted butter, softened
300 g/10 oz caster sugar
2 eggs
1 tsp almond essence
250 ml/8 fl oz milk
450 g/1 lb fresh blueberries

1. Preheat oven to 190°C/375°F/Gas Mark 5. Generously butter a 32 x 22 cm/13 x 9 inch ovenproof glass baking dish (do not use metal or porcelain). Prepare the streusel: Rub together all the ingredients until large crumbs form.

2. Prepare the filling: With an electric mixer, beat the cream cheese and sugar until creamy. Beat in the egg, lemon juice and almond essence.

3. Prepare the cake: Sift together the flour, baking powder and salt. With an electric mixer, beat the butter and sugar until creamy, about 3 minutes. Beat in the eggs, one at a time, beating well after each addition. Beat in the almond essence. On low speed, beat in the flour mixture alternately with the milk and ending with the flour mixture. Carefully fold in all the blueberries.

4. Spread slightly less than half the cake mixture over the bottom of the dish. Spread the filling over the batter. Sprinkle over one-quarter of the streusel topping. Drop spoonfuls of remaining batter over the top and spread evenly. Sprinkle on remaining topping. Bake 1 hour until crunchy and golden brown.

5. Remove to a wire rack and cool completely in the dish. Cut into squares and serve.

Chocolate-Almond Zuccotto

12–14 SERVINGS

Chocolate Roulade Cake (p. 24)
2 Tbsp almond-flavoured liqueur

CHOCOLATE-ALMOND FILLING

475 ml/16 fl oz double cream
450 g/1 lb ricotta cheese
100 g/4 oz granulated sugar
4 Tbsp almond-flavoured liqueur
175 g/6 oz plain chocolate, melted
75 g/3 oz plain chocolate, grated
50 g/2 oz chopped almonds, lightly toasted

CHOCOLATE WHIPPED CREAM

300 g/10 oz good-quality plain or bittersweet chocolate, chopped
475 ml/16 fl oz double cream
2 Tbsp almond-flavoured liqueur
50 g/2 oz chopped almonds, lightly toasted

1. Cool roulade. Cut out a 20 cm/8 inch circle from cake. Cut remaining long strip of cake into long narrow triangles, 5 cm/2 inches at base end and cut any remaining cake into pieces. Sprinkle with liqueur.

2. Line bowl with cling film, then with the point of each triangle in the centre of the bowl, line with the triangles; using any cake pieces to fill in gaps.

3. Beat the cream until stiff peaks form. Beat the ricotta with the sugar and liqueur. Stir a spoonful of cream into the ricotta, fold in remaining cream. Remove half the mixture to the "cream" bowl.

4. Fold the melted chocolate into one-half of the ricotta-cream mixture. Fold the grated chocolate and almonds into other half. Spoon the chocolate-almond mixture into cake-lined bowl and spread on base and up sides, covering the cake and smoothing the edges. Spoon the chocolate-ricotta mixture into centre. Cover with the 20 cm/8 inch cake round. Refrigerate overnight.

5. Prepare the chocolate cream: Heat the chocolate in a heatproof bowl set over a saucepan of just simmering water. Stir until melted and smooth. Cool. Beat the cream with the liqueur until soft peaks form and fold the chocolate into the cream.

6. Turn out on to a plate. Peel off the cling film and spread the chocolate cream over the top and sides. Sprinkle over the almonds and refrigerate.

Carrot Cake with Maple Cream Cheese

10–12 SERVINGS

175 g/6 oz plain flour
2 tsp baking powder
1/2 tsp bicarbonate of soda
1/2 tsp salt
2 tsp cinnamon
1 tsp ground allspice
1 tsp ground ginger
1 Tbsp grated orange rind
4 eggs
225 g/8 oz dark brown sugar
100 g/4 oz granulated sugar
300 ml/1/2 pt vegetable oil
1 Tbsp vanilla essence
450 g/1 lb sweet carrots, grated
100 g/4 oz chopped walnuts or pecans
75 g/3 oz raisins
75 g/3 oz sultanas

MAPLE CREAM CHEESE ICING

2 (225 g/8 oz) cartons cream cheese, softened
350 g/12 oz icing sugar, sifted
85 ml/3 fl oz maple syrup
2 to 4 Tbsp milk to dilute if necessary
175 g/6 oz finely chopped toasted walnuts for decoration (optional)

1. Preheat oven to 180°C/350°F/Gas Mark 4. Grease two 22 cm/9 inch cake tins. Line the bottoms with baking paper and regrease. Dust lightly with flour. Sift together the flour, baking powder, bicarbonate of soda, salt, cinnamon, allspice and ginger. Stir in the orange rind.

2. Beat eggs until blended. Add sugars and beat well. Slowly beat in the oil, then the vanilla essence. Stir in the flour mixture in three batches then stir in the carrots, walnuts or pecans, raisins and sultanas. Divide the batter between the tins. Bake 25 minutes. Cool in tins 10 minutes, then turn out on to a wire rack and cool completely. Remove paper.

3. Prepare the icing: With an electric mixer, beat the cream cheese. Gradually beat in the sugar until fluffy. Beat in maple syrup until spreadable. If necessary add a little milk to thin.

4. Put one cake layer on a plate, bottom-side down and spread with one-quarter of icing. Cover with second cake layer, rounded-side up. Spread top and side of cake with remaining icing. Decorate with walnuts. Refrigerate 1 hour to set the icing.

Chocolate Decadence

10–12 SERVINGS

CHOCOLATE MOUSSE CAKE

300 g/10 oz good-quality plain chocolate, chopped
100 g/4 oz unsalted butter
8 eggs, separated
50 ml/2 fl oz raspberry-flavoured liqueur
1/4 tsp cream of tartar

CHOCOLATE RASPBERRY GANACHE FILLING

350 g/12 oz good-quality plain chocolate, chopped
175 g/6 oz unsalted butter, cut into pieces
150 g/5 oz seedless raspberry jam
50 ml/2 fl oz raspberry-flavoured liqueur

CHOCOLATE-RASPBERRY GLAZE

250 ml/8 fl oz double cream
225 g/8 oz good-quality plain chocolate, chopped
2 Tbsp raspberry-flavoured liqueur
75 g/3 oz fresh raspberries for decoration
Icing sugar for dusting, sifted

1. Preheat oven to 180°C/350°F/Gas Mark 4. Lightly butter two 22 cm/9 inch springform tins. Line the bottoms with nonstick baking paper and butter the tins again.

2. Heat the chocolate and butter. Beat the egg yolks then gradually whisk into the melted chocolate. Whisk in the raspberry-flavoured liqueur.

3. Beat the egg whites until frothy. Add the cream of tartar and continue beating until soft peaks form. Fold the whites into the chocolate-egg mixture.

4. Divide the mixture evenly between the two tins. Bake 35 minutes. Remove cakes to a wire rack to cool for 15 minutes. Remove sides of the tins and cool cakes. Invert on to a rack, remove tin bottoms and peel off paper.

5. Heat the chocolate, butter and half the raspberry jam for the filling. Remove from heat and stir in half the raspberry-flavoured liqueur. Heat the remaining jam and liqueur. Spread a thin layer of the jam mixture over each cake layer.

6. Place one cake layer in cleaned tin, jam side up. Spread with filling. Top with second cake layer, jam-side down against filling. Refrigerate overnight.

7. Prepare the glaze: Bring the cream to a boil. Remove from heat and add in the chocolate all at once stirring until melted and smooth. Stir in the raspberry-flavoured liqueur and set aside to cool. Remove the side of the springform tin. Transfer the cake to a wire rack set over a baking sheet. Pour the glaze over the cake, smooth the top and sides and allow to set. Scrape remaining glaze off the baking sheet back into the bowl and whisk until smooth. Pipe a scroll border around the edge of cake. Decorate with raspberries and dust with icing sugar.

Cranberry-Orange Upside-Down Cake
with Orange Sauce

8 SERVINGS

"Upside-down" cakes became very popular in the 1940s, the most famous being made with tinned pineapple rings.

ORANGE SAUCE

1 Tbsp cornflour
250 ml/8 fl oz freshly squeezed orange juice, strained
Grated rind of 1 orange
50 g/2 oz granulated sugar
25 g/1 oz unsalted butter

CRANBERRY TOPPING

50 g/2 oz unsalted butter, melted
300 g/10 oz fresh cranberries
175 g/6 oz caster sugar
Grated rind of 1 orange
¼ tsp cinnamon

CAKE

75 g/3 oz plain flour
1 tsp baking powder
¼ tsp salt
3 eggs
100 g/4 oz sugar
½ tsp vanilla essence
Grated rind of 1 orange
45 g/1½ oz unsalted butter, melted

1. Prepare the orange sauce: Put the cornflour into a saucepan and whisk in the orange juice until the cornflour is dissolved. Whisk in the orange rind, sugar and add the butter, then bring to the boil, whisking constantly for 1 minute until thickened. Simmer about 2 minutes. Remove from heat and cool.

2. Preheat oven to 180°C/350°F/Gas Mark 4. Pour the melted butter into a 22 cm/9 inch cake tin. Mix the cranberries, sugar, orange rind and sugar. Spread over the bottom of the tin, pressing into the butter.

3. Sift the flour, baking powder and salt twice. Put the eggs in a heatproof bowl and place over a pan of simmering water. With an electric mixer, beat until frothy. Gradually beat in the sugar until thick and pale. Beat in the vanilla essence and orange rind.

4. Remove from heat and fold in the flour mixture in three batches; drizzle in the melted butter and fold into the batter. Spoon the batter over the cranberry layer. Bake 35 minutes. Remove to a wire rack to cool, about 7 minutes.

5. Run a knife around the edge of the tin to loosen the cake. Place a plate over the tin, bottom side up, and quickly turn out the cake. Serve with the sauce.

Rose Petal Jam Cake
with Strawberries

8 SERVINGS

100 g/4 oz plain flour
1 tsp baking powder
Pinch of salt
65 g/2½ oz unsalted butter, softened
100 g/4 oz caster sugar
1 large egg, lightly beaten
*3 Tbsp rose-water**
50 ml/2 fl oz milk
*150 g/5 oz rose petal jam**

ROSE-SCENTED WHIPPED CREAM

250 ml/8 fl oz double cream
1 Tbsp rose-water
1 Tbsp icing sugar, sifted
150 g/5 oz small or alpine strawberries

1. Preheat oven to 180°C/350°F/Gas Mark 4. Grease and flour a 22 cm/9 inch cake tin. In a large bowl sift together the flour, baking powder and salt.

2. With an electric mixer, beat the butter and sugar until light and creamy, 5 minutes. Gradually beat in the egg and a tablespoon of rose-water. Beat in the flour mixture and the milk alternately in three batches ending with the flour mixture.

3. Scrape the batter into the prepared tin. Bake about 25 minutes or until done. Remove to a wire rack and cool in the tin 5 minutes. Turn out cake top-side up on to the wire rack to cool completely.

4. Split cake into two layers. Drizzle a tablespoon of rose-water over each cut surface. Allow to soak in for a few minutes. Lightly beat the jam and spread on to the cut-side of the bottom half of the cake.

5. With an electric mixer beat the cream with the rose-water and icing sugar. Spread about half the whipped cream over the jam and sprinkle with half of the strawberries. Top with the second cake layer rounded-side up and spread the remaining cream over the top swirling decoratively; sprinkle over remaining strawberries and dust with a little more icing sugar. This cake is best eaten the same day that it is made.

*Rose-water and rose petal jam can be found in some large supermarkets, specialist stores and Middle Eastern grocery shops.

Christmas Fruit Cake

16 SERVINGS

This is a delicious, moist fruit cake that keeps well; it is ideal for the holiday season. After tasting this cake at a friend's house, I begged for the recipe from her Auntie Margaret who sent it from Co. Monaghan.

200 g/7 oz self-raising flour
1 tsp bicarbonate of soda
1 tsp cinnamon
1 tsp mixed spice
1 tsp ground ginger
1/4 tsp salt
100 g/4 oz butter
75 g/3 oz soft brown sugar
1 (400 g/13½ oz) can crushed pineapple
150 g/5 oz raisins
150 g/5 oz sultanas
150 g/5 oz currants
100 g/4 oz crystallized ginger, finely chopped
100 g/4 oz glacé cherries, chopped
50 g/2 oz mixed candied peel
2 eggs, lightly beaten
Pecan halves for decoration (optional)
Glacé cherries, halved, for decoration (optional)
2 to 3 Tbsp honey or marmalade for glazing

1. Sift the flour, baking soda, cinnamon, mixed spice, ground ginger and salt into a bowl and set aside. Melt the butter and sugar in a saucepan until the sugar has dissolved, stirring frequently.

2. Add the pineapple with its juices and stir in the dried fruits and ginger. Bring to the boil and simmer 3 minutes, stirring. Remove from heat and cool.

3. Preheat oven to 170°C/325°F/Gas Mark 3. Grease a 20 x 7.5 cm/8 x 3 inch nonstick cake tin with a removeable bottom. Line the bottom and sides with baking paper; regrease and lightly flour.

4. When cool, add the fruit mixture to the flour mixture with the glacé cherries and mixed peel. Stir in the beaten eggs and spoon into the tin and smooth the top. Arrange circles of pecan and cherry halves on the top pressing gently into the batter.

5. Bake 1 hour 20 minutes or until a skewer inserted into the centre comes out clean. If cake colours too quickly, lower the temperature slightly and cover the top with a piece of foil. Remove to a wire rack to cool 30 minutes before turning out. Turn cake right-side up and cool completely. Melt the honey or marmalade and brush over the top.

Chocolate Roulade
with White Chocolate Cream and Black Cherry Compote

12–14 SERVINGS

This cake is based on the classic Black Forest Cake – a combination of a rich dark chocolate roulade filled with a luscious white chocolate cream and served with a fresh cherry compote.

BLACK CHERRY COMPOTE
175 ml/6 fl oz water
75 g/3 oz granulated sugar
2 Tbsp fresh lemon or orange juice
1 vanilla pod, halved lengthways or
1 Tbsp vanilla essence
450 g/1 lb fresh black cherries, stoned and halved if you like

CHOCOLATE GANACHE ICING
300 ml/½ pt double cream
350 g/12 oz plain or bittersweet chocolate, chopped
2 Tbsp Kirsch or cognac

CAKE
5 eggs, separated
3 Tbsp cocoa powder, plus extra for dusting, sifted
Pinch of cream of tartar
150 g/5 oz icing sugar, plus extra for dusting, sifted

WHITE CHOCOLATE CREAM FILLING
200 g/7 oz good-quality white chocolate, chopped
475 ml/16 fl oz double cream
2 Tbsp Kirsch

1. Prepare the compote: In a saucepan combine the water, sugar, lemon, or orange juice and vanilla pod or essence. Bring to the boil, stirring until the sugar has dissolved. Boil 3–4 minutes until thickened, then stir in the cherries. Simmer 1 minute. Cool. Remove the vanilla pod and pour compote into a bowl. Cover and refrigerate.

2. Prepare the icing: Bring the cream to the boil. Remove from heat and add the chocolate all at once, stirring until melted. Strain into a bowl, stir in the Kirsch or cognac and cool. Refrigerate at least 2 hours or until set.

3. Prepare the cake: Preheat oven to 200°C/400°F/Gas Mark 6. Grease a 39 x 26 cm/15½ x 10½ inch swiss roll tin and line with nonstick baking paper. With an electric mixer, beat the egg yolks until thick and creamy, about 5 minutes. Beat in the cocoa and half the icing sugar. Set aside.

4. Beat the egg whites until frothy. Add the cream of tartar and beat until soft peaks form. Add the remaining icing sugar 2 tablespoons at a time, beating well until stiff and glossy. Stir a spoonful of the whites into the yolk mixture, then gently fold the yolk mixture into the whites and spread the batter into the tin. Bake about 15 minutes.

5. Lay a clean dish towel on a work surface and cover with nonstick baking paper, dust with cocoa or icing sugar. Turn cake on to paper and peel off the lining paper. Starting from one narrow end, roll cake with the paper and towel, swiss roll fashion. Cool on a wire rack.

6. Prepare the filling: Over low heat, heat the white chocolate with 120 ml/4 fl oz of the cream until melted. Strain and cool. Beat the remaining cream with the Kirsch until soft peaks form. Stir a spoonful of the cream into the white chocolate mixture then fold it into the remaining cream.

7. To assemble: Unroll the cooled cake and spread with the white chocolate cream. Reroll the cake without the paper. Transfer to a serving plate. Beat icing until slightly lightened in colour and texture, about 30 seconds; do not overbeat. Spread over the roulade. Dust with icing sugar and serve with the compote.

CHAPTER TWO

PIES, PASTRIES and TARTS

Basic Sweet Shortcrust Pastry

100 g/4 oz plain flour
½ tsp salt
3 to 4 Tbsp icing sugar, sifted
100 g/4 oz cold unsalted butter (8 Tbsp), cut into small pieces
2 egg yolks
2 Tbsp iced water
½ tsp vanilla essence (optional)

VARIATION "EXTRA SWEET TART PASTRY"
100 g/4 oz plain flour
½ tsp salt
4 to 5 Tbsp icing sugar, sifted
100 g/4 oz cold unsalted butter (8 Tbsp), cut into small pieces
3 egg yolks
1 Tbsp iced water

1. Process the flour, salt and sugar in a food processor for 5 seconds. Sprinkle the butter over the flour mixture and process about 15 seconds until the mixture resembles coarse crumbs.

2. Beat the egg yolks with the iced water and vanilla and with the machine running, through the feed tube. Process until the dough just begins to hold together. DO NOT OVERPROCESS. Test by pinching a piece of dough between your fingers. If it is still crumbly add a little more water and pulse once or twice. Do not allow dough to form into a ball or the pastry will be tough. Turn out on to a sheet of cling film.

3. Using the cling film as a guide, hold each side with one hand and gently push the dough away from you, turning the dough and holding the opposite sides of the cling film to contain the dough, until the dough is smooth and just blended. Flatten into a disc shape and wrap with the cling film. Refrigerate 1 hour or overnight. Allow pastry to soften slightly at room temperature before using.

Crumb Crust

Ideal for chilled tarts. Particularly good for ice cream tarts and chilled mixtures. Use vanilla, chocolate, amaretti biscuits (about 24) or ginger biscuits (24–26) instead of digestives or replace 50g/2oz cup of crumbs with 50 g/2 oz finely-chopped nuts for a nut crust.

FOR ONE 22 CM/9 INCH TART CASE
225 g/8 oz digestive biscuits (about 18–20) or other biscuit crumbs
75 g/3 oz butter or margarine, melted
1 to 2 Tbsp caster sugar (optional)

1. Put the biscuits in a food processor and process 20–30 seconds until fine crumbs form. Alternatively, put them in a heavy-duty freezer bag and press into fine crumbs with a rolling pin. Pour into a bowl and stir in the butter and sugar. Pour into a tart tin and press on to bottom and up sides. Chill 20 minutes.

2. Preheat oven to 190°C/375°F/Gas Mark 5. Bake 6–8 minutes until set. Remove to wire rack to cool.

Cream Cheese Pastry

This is a moist, flaky pastry often used with sugary or nutty fillings. It is ideal for rich tartlets and tiny petits fours.

FOR ONE 9 INCH TART CASE OR TWELVE 2 OR 3 INCH TARTLETS
100 g/4 oz plain flour
½ tsp salt
1 tsp caster sugar
100 g/4 oz unsalted butter, at room temperature
100 g/4 oz full fat cream cheese, at room temperature

1. In a large bowl, sift together the flour and salt. With an electric mixer add the butter and cream cheese and beat the ingredients together until blended and a soft dough forms. Roll into a ball, flatten to a disc shape, and wrap tightly. Refrigerate about 1 hour before rolling and shaping.

Chocolate Pastry

This is a wonderfully rich, sweet pastry, almost like a chocolate biscuit. It makes a stunning base for fruit tarts and tartlets and anything that goes well with chocolate.

MAKES ONE 9 OR 10 INCH TART CASE

100 g/4 oz unsalted butter, softened
75 g/3 oz caster sugar
1/2 tsp salt
2 tsp vanilla essence
50 g/2 oz cocoa powder
175 g/6 oz plain flour

1. Put the butter, sugar, salt and vanilla in a food processor and process 25–30 seconds until creamy. Add the cocoa and process 1 minute. Add all of the flour and, process for 15 seconds until the flour is well blended. Scrape dough on to a sheet of cling film and shape into a flat disc. Wrap tightly and refrigerate 1 hour or overnight.

2. Soften the dough 10 minutes at room temperature. Unwrap and turn on to a large clean piece of cling film; cover with another piece of cling film. Carefully roll out to about a 27 cm/11 inch round about 1/2–1 cm/1/4 inch thick. Peel off top sheet and invert dough into a prepared tin. Gently ease dough on to bottom and side of tin, then remove the bottom layer of cling film. Press dough to the bottom and sides of tin, then roll rolling pin over the top of the tin to cut off any excess dough. Prick the base with a fork and refrigerate for 1 hour.

Creamy Rice Pudding Tartlets

6–8 SERVINGS

For rice-pudding lovers, this is the ultimate recipe: a creamy orange-scented version baked in a rich sweet pastry shell – a wonderful winter dessert.

8 (7.5 cm/3 inch) tartlets lined with Extra-Sweet Tart Pastry (p. 26), baked blind
150 g/5 oz Arborio (short-grain) rice
350 ml/12 fl oz milk
120 ml/4 fl oz freshly squeezed orange juice
1 tsp grated orange rind
225 g/8 oz granualted sugar
120 ml/4 fl oz double cream
2 eggs
2 egg yolks
2 Tbsp orange-flavoured liqueur or 1 tsp vanilla essence
Icing sugar for dusting, sifted
Whipped cream for serving (optional)

1. Preheat oven to 190°C/375°F/Gas Mark 5. Put the rice in a medium saucepan with the milk. Bring to the boil over medium-high heat, reduce heat to medium-low and cook, stirring constantly, until the rice is tender and milk is absorbed, 20 minutes.

2. Stir in the orange juice, rind and sugar and cook, stirring constantly, until the sugar is dissolved and juice is absorbed, about 5 minutes longer. Remove from heat and cool slightly.

3. Beat in the cream, eggs, egg yolks and liqueur or vanilla essence and divide the mixture among the tartlet cases. Set on a baking sheet for easier handling. Bake until pudding mixture is just set, 15–20 minutes. Remove to a wire rack to cool. Dust with icing sugar and serve warm, or cold with whipped cream if you like.

Tarte Tatin
with Crème Fraîche-Honey Swirl

8 SERVINGS

This famous French apple dessert is really an easy upside-down apple tart.

350 g/12 oz bought puff pastry or 1 quantity Basic Sweet Shortcrust Pastry (p. 26)

10 Golden Delicious apples, peeled and cored
Juice of 1 lemon
75 g/3 oz unsalted butter
175 g/6 oz granulated sugar
1/4 tsp cinnamon

CREME FRAICHE-HONEY SWIRL
350 ml/12 fl oz crème fraîche or soured cream
175 g/6 oz good-quality honey

1. On a lightly floured surface, roll out the pastry to a 27 cm/11 inch round, 1/2–1 cm/1/4 inch thick. Slide on to a lightly floured baking sheet and refrigerate until needed.

2. Halve the apples, sprinkle with lemon juice.

3. Melt the butter in a 25 cm/10 inch heavy-bottomed frying pan over medium-high heat. Add the sugar and cinnamon, stirring until the sugar dissolves. Cook, stirring until a golden caramel colour. Remove from heat. Do not touch the caramel – it is dangerously hot.

4. Arrange the apple halves closely in circles around the outside edge and centre of the pan.

5. Return the apple-filled pan to the heat and bring to the boil. Simmer until the apples begin to soften and the caramel darkens, about 20 minutes. Remove from heat to cool slightly.

6. Preheat oven to 220°C/425°F/Gas Mark 7. Soften the pastry, about 5 minutes. Slide the rolled-out dough round over the apple-filled dish, tucking the overhanging dough inside the edge. Pierce in two or three places. Bake about 25–30 minutes.

7. Prepare the crème fraîche-honey swirl: Spoon half the crème fraîche into a serving bowl. Drizzle half the honey over it, then spoon over the remaining cream and drizzle over the remaining honey. Gently draw a knife through the cream in a swirling pattern.

8. Cool the tarte tatin on a wire rack, about 5 minutes. Run a knife around the edge of the dish to release any pastry which might be stuck. Carefully turn out on to a plate and serve warm with the Crème Fraîche-Honey Swirl.

Summer Berry Strudel

6–8 SERVINGS

This is a delicious summer recipe – the almond cream adds a distinctive richness and flavour.

ALMOND CREAM

100 g/4 oz blanched almonds
50 g/2 oz granulated sugar
2 Tbsp plain flour
75 g/3 oz unsalted butter, softened and cut into pieces
1 egg
1 egg yolk
1/2 tsp almond essence

STRUDEL

175 g/6 oz butter, melted
150 g/5 oz fresh breadcrumbs
900 g/2 lb mixed summer berries, such as raspberries, blueberries, strawberries (hulled and chopped), plus extra for serving
100 g/4 oz granulated sugar plus extra for sprinkling
Grated rind of 1 lemon
8 large sheets filo pastry
Icing sugar for dusting, sifted
Whipped cream or crème fraîche for serving

1. Prepare the almond cream: Process the almonds, sugar and flour in a food processor until finely ground. Add the butter a few pieces at a time and process until creamy. Add the egg, egg yolk and almond essence and process until well blended.

2. Prepare the strudel: Heat 5 tablespoons of the melted butter in a large frying pan. Add the breadcrumbs and stir-fry for 5 minutes.

3. Preheat oven to 190°C/375°F/Gas Mark 5. Grease a large baking sheet. Toss the berries in a large bowl with 100 g/4 oz sugar and the lemon rind.

4. Place a filo pastry sheet on the work surface. Brush with melted butter and sprinkle with 15 g/1/2 oz of the breadcrumbs. Lay a second sheet of pastry over the top and repeat. Continue layering remaining filo sheets with butter and crumbs.

5. Spread the almond cream over the stack of pastry. Spoon the berry mixture over the centre and roll up in swiss roll fashion. Slide the strudel, seam-side down, on to the baking sheet. Brush with any remaining butter and sprinkle with a little sugar.

6. Bake about 45 minutes until crisp; cover with foil if it browns too quickly. Cool on a wire rack. Dust with icing sugar and serve with whipped cream or crème fraîche and extra berries.

Lemon Meringue Pie

6–8 SERVINGS

This delicious old-fashioned pie is an eternal favourite. The creamy yet sharp lemon custard and the light sweet meringue combine to make an elegant dessert.

1 (22 cm/9 inch) tart case lined with Basic Sweet Shortcrust Pastry (p. 26), baked blind
25 g/1 oz cornflour
1/8 tsp salt
300 g/10 oz granulated sugar
350 ml/12 fl oz water
4 eggs, separated
15 g/1/2 oz butter, diced
Grated rind of 1 large lemon
120 ml/4 fl oz freshly squeezed lemon juice (2 to 3 lemons)
1/4 tsp cream of tartar

1. In a saucepan, combine the cornflour, salt and 175 g/6 oz sugar. Gradually stir in the water and bring to the boil, stirring constantly until thickened; boil 1 minute more. Remove from heat.

2. Beat the egg yolks. Stir in a little of the hot cornflour mixture, then stir the egg mixture back into the cornflour mixture in the saucepan and return to the heat. Cook about 5 minutes, stirring constantly and rapidly to prevent lumps, until very thick. Remove from heat and beat in the butter, then gradually stir in the lemon rind and juice and pour into the prepared tart case.

3. Preheat oven to 190°C/375°F/Gas Mark 5. With an electric mixer, beat the egg whites and cream of tartar until soft peaks form. Gradually sprinkle in the remaining 100 g/4 oz sugar, a tablespoon at a time, beating well after each addition, until the whites form stiff peaks and the sugar is completely dissolved (test by rubbing a small amount between your thumb and index finger – it should feel smooth, not gritty).

4. Spoon the meringue on to the lemon mixture spreading to the edge of the crust to seal. Swirl with the back of a spoon to form a decorative pattern. Bake until meringue is just golden, 10 minutes. Transfer to a wire rack to cool completely. Serve the pie the same day.

WARNING: *This recipe contains lightly cooked egg whites.*

Black Bottom Tart

6–8 SERVINGS

This is an old-fashioned American pie with a new twist. Baked in a tart case and covered with chocolate whipped cream and chocolate curls, it becomes an elegant extravaganza.

1 (22 cm/9 inch) tart case lined with Chocolate Pastry (p. 27), or Ginger Crumb Crust (p. 26), baked blind
2 tsp unflavoured gelatine
3 Tbsp cold water
475 ml/16 fl oz milk
2 eggs, separated
1 egg yolk
175 g/6 oz granulated sugar
2 Tbsp cornflour
50 g/2 oz plain chocolate, chopped
3 to 4 Tbsp rum
1/4 tsp cream of tartar
250 ml/8 fl oz double cream
Chocolate curls or grated chocolate for decoration (optional)

1. In a small bowl or ramekin, sprinkle the gelatine evenly over the water and set aside to soften.

2. Bring the milk to the boil. Beat the egg yolks and half the sugar about 1 minute until light. Stir in the cornflour until just blended. Pour the hot milk over the egg yolk mixture, whisking constantly.

3. Return the custard to the heat and cook, whisking constantly, until the custard thickens and boils, about 2 minutes. Remove from heat and pour 250 ml/8 fl oz of the custard into a bowl and immediately stir in the chocolate until melted and smooth. Stir in half the rum and pour into the tart case to set.

4. Pour the softened gelatine into the remaining custard in the saucepan and stir until dissolved. Stir in the rum and refrigerate until the mixture begins to cool and thicken slightly.

5. With an electric mixer, beat the egg whites and cream of tartar until soft peaks form. Gradually beat in the remaining sugar a tablespoon at a time, beating well after each addition until stiff peaks form. Gently fold a spoonful of whites into the setting custard, then fold in the remaining whites and spoon into the tart case smoothing the top evenly. Refrigerate at least 2 hours until set.

6. Whip the cream and spoon over the tart making decorative swirls with the back of a spoon or knife. Decorate with chocolate curls or grated chocolate and serve chilled.

California Prune Linzer Tart

6–8 SERVINGS

This biscuit-like tart is popular in Eastern Europe. Dried apricots or fresh cherries can be substituted for prunes.

350 g/12 oz ready-to-eat stoned prunes
Grated rind and juice of 1 orange
175 ml/6 fl oz water
2 Tbsp granulated sugar
1/2 tsp cinnamon
1/2 tsp almond essence

CHOCOLATE-ALMOND PASTRY

75 g/3 oz blanched almonds
175 g/6 oz caster sugar
175 g/6 oz plain flour, sifted
2 Tbsp cocoa powder, sifted
1 tsp cinnamon
1/2 tsp salt
Grated rind of 1 orange
225 g/8 oz unsalted butter, cut into pieces
2 to 3 Tbsp iced water
Icing sugar for dusting, sifted

1. Bring the prunes to a boil with the orange rind and juice and water. Simmer until the liquid is absorbed and the prunes soft and plump, 15 minutes. Stir in the sugar and the cinnamon and almond essence. Process in a food processor, 20–30 seconds. Cover and chill.

2. Spray or butter a 27 cm/11 inch tart tin. Process the almonds and half the sugar to fine crumbs. Add the remaining sugar, flour, cocoa, cinnamon, salt and orange rind and process to blend. Add the butter and process until coarse crumbs form, about 20 seconds. Add the water a tablespoon at a time and process until the dough just begins to form.

3. Turn the dough on to a large piece of cling film and knead lightly. Press half the dough on to the bottom and sides of the tin. Prick the bottom and refrigerate 30 minutes. Roll out the remaining dough and cut into 1 cm/1/2 inch strips.

4. Preheat oven to 190°C/375°F/Gas Mark 5. Spread the prune filling on to the pastry-lined tart tin. Arrange the dough strips on the top in a lattice pattern. Bake about 35 minutes. Cool then dust with icing sugar.

Pear and Chocolate Cream Tart

6–8 SERVINGS

1 (22 cm/9 inch) tart case lined with Chocolate Pastry (p. 27)
100 g/4 oz plain chocolate, melted
250 ml/8 fl oz double cream
50 g/2 oz granulated sugar
1 egg
1 egg yolk
1 tsp vanilla or almond essence
3 medium ripe pears

1. Melt the chocolate, cream and 2 tablespoons of the sugar, stirring frequently, until smooth. Remove from heat and cool slightly. Beat in the egg, egg yolk and vanilla and set aside.

2. Preheat oven to 190°C/375°F/Gas Mark 5. Peel, halve and core the pears. Put them on a work surface cut-side down and cut across into thin slices.

3. Arrange the pears spoke-fashion in the tart and press gently with your hand to carefully fan out the pear slices toward the centre. Slowly pour the chocolate mixture between the pears, trying to leave the pears uncovered. Tap gently on the work surface to eliminate any air bubbles.

4. Bake 10 minutes. Reduce oven to 180°C/350°F/Gas Mark 4. Sprinkle the tart with the remaining sugar and bake until the custard is set and pears are tender and glazed, about another 20 minutes. Transfer to a wire rack to cool slightly. Serve warm.

VARIATION: *one 22 cm/9 inch tart case lined with Extra-Sweet Tart Crust (p. 28). Spread with the Almond Cream from Summer Berry Strudel (p. 31). Arrange the pears as above, baking about 45 minutes until pears are tender.*

Rich Nectarine Tart

6–8 SERVINGS

This tart is equally delicious made with plums or peaches.

RICH PASTRY

175 g/6 oz plain flour
75 g/3 oz granulated sugar
½ tsp cinnamon
100 g/4 oz butter at room temperature, cut into small pieces

NECTARINE FILLING

675 g/1½ lb nectarines
½ tsp almond essence
2 to 3 Tbsp sugar
2 Tbsp plain flour
½ tsp cinnamon
25 g/1 oz slivered almonds

1. Preheat oven to 190°C/375°F/Gas Mark 5. Lightly spray or oil a 22 cm/9 inch tart tin.

2. Stir together the flour, sugar and cinnamon. Sprinkle over the pieces of butter and using a pastry blender, cut in the butter until a soft dough begins to form. Pour into the tart case and, using your fingertips, press the dough evenly on to the bottom and up the sides of the tin. Set aside.

3. Cut the nectarines in half and scoop out each stone. Cut into 1 cm/½ inch slices. Toss the nectarines with almond essence, sugar (depending on the sweetness of fruit), flour and cinnamon. Starting at the outside edge, arrange the slices in overlapping concentric circles and sprinkle with the almonds.

4. Set the tart case on a baking sheet and bake until the nectarines are tender and pastry is golden and crisp, 40 minutes. Rotate the tart halfway through cooking if it begins to colour unevenly. Transfer to a wire rack to cool. Serve warm.

Chocolate Profiteroles

4–6 SERVINGS

This mouthwatering dessert is served in cafés throughout France. Sometimes the profiteroles are filled with whipped or pastry cream but they are always drizzled with chocolate sauce.

PROFITEROLES
75 g/3 oz plain flour
¼ tsp salt
Pinch of freshly grated nutmeg
175 ml/6 fl oz water
75 g/3 oz unsalted butter, cut into 6 pieces
3 eggs

CHOCOLATE SAUCE
300 g/10 oz plain chocolate
120 ml/4 fl oz warm water
750 ml/1¼ pt vanilla ice cream

1. Prepare the profiteroles: Preheat oven to 200°C/400°F/Gas Mark 6 and butter a large baking sheet. Sift together the flour, salt and nutmeg. In a saucepan, bring the water and butter to a boil. Remove from heat and add the flour mixture all at once. Beat with a wooden spoon for 1 minute until well blended and the mixture starts to pull away from the sides of the pan. Place over a low heat and cook for about 2 minutes, beating constantly. Remove from heat.

2. Beat an egg in a small bowl and set aside. Add the remaining eggs, one at a time, to the flour mixture, beating well after each addition. Add the beaten egg by teaspoonfuls until the dough is smooth and shiny; it should pull away and fall slowly when dropped from a spoon.

3. Using a tablespoon, drop the dough on to the baking sheet in 12 mounds. Bake 25–30 minutes until well risen and browned. Turn off the oven and leave the puffs to cool with the oven door open.

4. Prepare the sauce: Put the chocolate and water in a small saucepan. Melt over medium heat, stirring frequently until melted and smooth. Keep warm until ready to serve, or reheat, over simmering water. Split the profiteroles in half and put a small scoop of ice cream in each. Arrange on a serving platter or divide among individual plates. Pour the chocolate sauce over the top and serve at once.

Lemon Tart

6–8 SERVINGS

1 (22–25 cm/9 or 10 inch) tart case lined with Extra-Sweet Tart Crust (p. 26), partially baked blind
Grated rind of 2 to 3 lemons
150 ml/¼ pt freshly-squeezed lemon juice
175 g/6 oz granulated sugar
120 ml/4 fl oz double cream or crème fraîche
3 eggs
3 egg yolks
Icing sugar for dusting, sifted

1. Preheat oven to 190°C/375°F/Gas Mark 5. With an electric mixer on low speed, beat the lemon rind, juice and sugar. Slowly beat in the cream or crème fraîche until well blended, then beat in the eggs and yolks, one at a time.

2. Set the tart case on a baking sheet for easier handling and carefully pour in the filling. (If you prefer a completely smooth filling, strain into the tart case, removing the rind.)

3. Bake until the filling is just set, but not coloured, about 20 minutes. If the tart begins to colour, cover with foil. Remove to a wire rack to cool completely. Dust with icing sugar before serving.

Lime Curd Filo Tartlets
with Raspberry Sauce

6–8 SERVINGS

These crisp filo cups make a stunning container for a soft tangy lime curd filling. The raspberry sauce adds a sharp colour as well as good flavour contrast.

4 sheets filo pastry, defrosted if frozen
25 g/1 oz unsalted butter, melted
caster sugar
2 eggs, beaten
100 g/4 oz unsalted butter, diced
100 g/4 oz granulated sugar
2 Tbsp freshly grated lime rind
50 ml/2 fl oz freshly squeezed lime juice (about 2 limes)
450 g/1 lb fresh raspberries

1. Preheat oven to 180°C/350°F/Gas Mark 4. Lightly spray or oil four 175 ml/6 fl oz ramekins with vegetable spray or oil. Stack the filo pastry sheets on a work surface and cut into 15 cm/6 inch squares. Keep the filo pastry covered with a damp cloth to prevent the dough from drying out.

2. Place a filo square on the work surface, brush with a little melted butter and sprinkle with a little sugar. Butter a second square and lay it over the first square at an angle; sprinkle with a little sugar. Repeat with two more filo squares, placing at different angles to create an uneven edge. Press the stack of squares into a ramekin pressing into the edge and keeping the edges turned up. Continue to line the remaining ramekins.

3. Set the ramekins on a baking sheet for easier handling and bake until crisp and golden, about 8 minutes. (Watch carefully, as the edges can burn easily.) Transfer to a wire rack and cool completely.

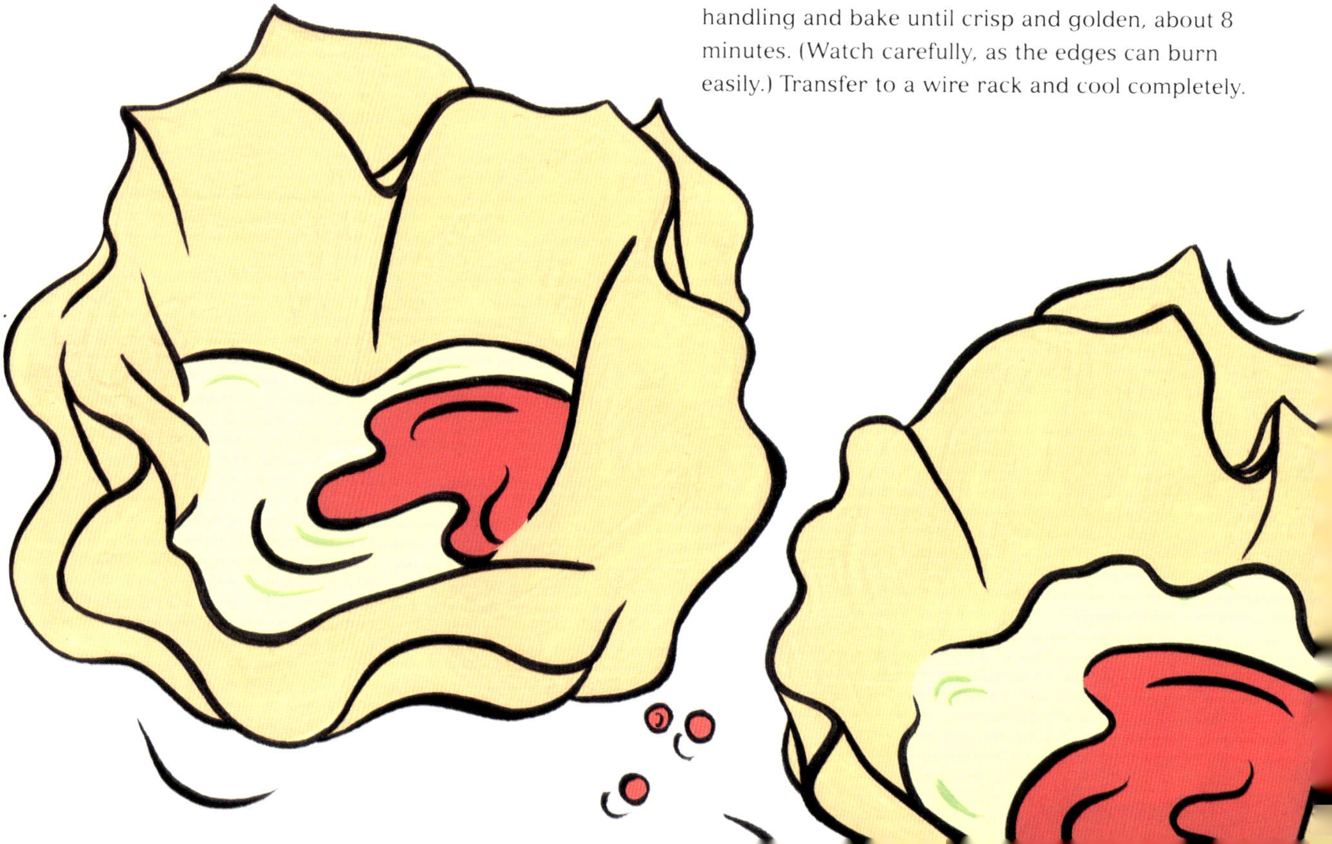

4. In a saucepan, combine the eggs, butter, 100 g/4 oz sugar, lime rind and juice and cook, over medium-low heat, until the mixture begins to thicken and bubbles begin to appear on the surface, about 3 minutes. Scrape into a bowl and cover with cling film, pressing film against the surface of the curd to prevent a skin from forming. Refrigerate at least 1 hour. Stir before using.

5. Put half the raspberries and 2–3 tablespoons of sugar in a food processor and process until smooth. Strain into a bowl and stir in remaining berries. Just before serving, divide the curd mixture evenly among the filo cups and top each with some of the sauce; serve remaining sauce separately. Decorate with mint.

Lemon Blueberry Napoleons with Blueberry Sauce

6–8 SERVINGS

This elegant dessert is a classic combination of puff pastry, lemon pastry cream and sweet succulent blueberries.

BLUEBERRY SAUCE

450 g/ 1 lb blueberries
75 g/3 oz sugar to taste
2 to 3 Tbsp freshly squeezed lemon juice
2 to 3 Tbsp water

PASTRY CREAM

6 egg yolks
75 g/3 oz granulated sugar
Grated rind of 1 lemon
3 Tbsp plain flour
350 ml/12 fl oz milk
½ tsp lemon or vanilla essence

450 g/1 lb bought puff pastry, defrosted if frozen
50 ml/2 fl oz double cream, whipped
450 g/ 1 lb blueberries
Icing sugar for dusting, sifted
Fresh mint sprigs for decoration (optional)

1. Prepare the sauce: Process the blueberries, sugar, lemon juice and water in a food processor for 1 minute. Strain through a nonmetallic strainer into a bowl and taste for sweetness. Add a little more sugar if necessary. Cover and refrigerate.

2. Prepare the pastry cream: Put the yolks, sugar and lemon rind in a bowl and whisk until creamy, about 2 minutes. Gently stir in the flour. Bring the milk to the boil. Pour half the milk over the yolk mixture, whisking vigorously. Return to the saucepan and boil 2 minutes, whisking constantly until thickened and smooth. Stir in the lemon or vanilla essence. Remove from heat and cool.

3. Oil a large baking sheet. On a lightly floured surface, roll out the pastry into a rectangle at least 40 x 30 cm/16 x 12 inches; cut four strips 10 cm/4 inches wide and about 30 cm/12 inches long. Transfer to the baking sheet. Prick with a fork and chill for about 30 minutes. Preheat oven to 200°C/400°F/Gas Mark 6. Bake the pastry strips 20 minutes until crisp and golden. Cool completely on a wire rack.

4. Beat the whipped cream into the pastry cream. Spread one pastry strip with one-third of the pastry cream and sprinkle with blueberries. Top with a second strip, spread with more pastry cream and blueberries. Repeat. Dust the top pastry strips with icing sugar. Decorate with mint and serve with the blueberry sauce.

Pumpkin Tart
with Crunchy Walnut Topping

6–8 SERVINGS

1 (22 cm/9 inch) tart case lined with Basic Sweet Shortcrust Pastry (p. 26), partially baked blind
400 g/14 oz tinned pumpkin
100 g/4 oz granulated sugar
50 g/2 oz soft brown sugar
175 ml/6 fl oz double cream
85 ml/3 fl oz milk
2 eggs
1 to 2 Tbsp whisky (optional)
3/4 tsp cinnamon
1/2 tsp allspice
1/2 tsp ground ginger
1/4 tsp ground cloves
1/4 tsp ground nutmeg

TOPPING

50 g/2 oz chopped walnuts or pecans
100 g/4 oz soft brown sugar
25 g/1 oz unsalted butter, melted
Whipped cream or vanilla ice-cream for serving

1. Preheat oven to 180°C/350°F/Gas Mark 4. With an electric mixer, beat the pumpkin with the remaining ingredients (except those for the topping and the whipped cream) until smooth and well blended. Set the tart on a baking sheet for easier handling and carefully pour the mixture into the tart case.

2. Bake until the filling is just set and the pastry is golden brown, about 45 minutes. Cover the pastry edges with a piece of foil if it browns too quickly. Carefully, remove the tart to a wire rack to cool.

3. Preheat the grill. Combine the walnuts or pecans, sugar and butter and sprinkle evenly over the tart. Cover the edge of the pastry with a strip of foil. Grill about 10 cm/4 inches from the heat until the topping bubbles and caramelizes, watching carefully, about 1 minute. Allow to cool then serve.

Double Chocolate Truffle Tarts

6–8 SERVINGS

A chocolate lover's fantasy: Chocolate pastry filled with rich truffle and dusted with cocoa.

8 (10 cm/4 inch) tartlet tins lined with Chocolate Pastry (p. 27), baked blind
300 ml/10 fl oz double cream
300 g/10 oz plain chocolate, chopped
2 Tbsp unsalted butter
50 ml/2 fl oz cognac or favourite liqueur
Cocoa powder for dusting, sifted

1. In a medium saucepan over medium-high heat, bring the cream to the boil. Remove from heat and add all the chocolate, stirring until completely melted and smooth. Beat in the butter and stir in the cognac or liqueur to taste. Strain the mixture into a measuring cup or jug.

2. Divide the mixture evenly among the tartlet cases, smoothing the tops so they are completely flat. Refrigerate 3–4 hours or overnight.

3. Cut out strips of greaseproof paper about 6 mm/3/8 inch wide. Place in a random pattern over each tartlet and dust with cocoa. Refrigerate until ready to serve. Allow to soften 15 minutes before serving.

Chocolate Truffle and Berry Tart
with Raspberry Cream

6–8 SERVINGS

Summer berries are the perfect foil for a rich chocolate tart case filled with a dark chocolate and raspberry truffle mixture.

1 (22 cm/9 inch) tart case lined with Chocolate Pastry (p. 27), baked blind
400 ml/14 fl oz double cream
300 g/10 oz seedless raspberry jam
225 g/8 oz good-quality plain chocolate, chopped
50 ml/2 fl oz Framboise or other raspberry-flavoured liqueur
675 g/1½ lb mixed fresh summer berries, such as raspberries, blackberries, strawberries (quartered if large) or blueberries
250 ml/8 fl oz double cream
1 to 2 Tbsp caster sugar

1. Bring the cream and three-quarters of the raspberry jam to the boil, whisking to dissolve the jam. Remove from heat and add all the chocolate, stirring until melted and smooth. Strain the mixture into the tart case, tilting and turning the tart to distribute the filling evenly. Refrigerate until set.

2. In a saucepan over medium heat, heat the remaining raspberry jam and 2 tablespoons of the liqueur until melted and bubbling. Drizzle over the berries and toss to coat well. Arrange the berries over the top. Refrigerate until ready to serve.

3. Bring to room temperature at least 30 minutes before serving. Whip the cream with the sugar and remaining liqueur until soft peaks form. Spoon into a serving bowl and serve with the tart.

Key Lime Pie
with Pineau des Charentes Cream and Chocolate Sauce

6–8 SERVINGS

1 (22 cm/9 inch) pie dish lined with Ginger Crumb Crust (p. 26)

KEY LIME PIE

3 large egg yolks
1 (400 g/14 oz) tin sweetened condensed milk
120 ml/4 fl oz Key lime or freshly squeezed lime juice (about 3 medium limes)
1 Tbsp grated lime rind

PINEAU DES CHARENTES CREAM

300 ml/½ pt double cream
50 g/2 oz caster sugar
2 to 3 Tbsp Pineau des Charentes or other sweet dessert wine

CHOCOLATE SAUCE

100 g/4 oz good-quality plain or bittersweet chocolate, chopped
85 ml/3 fl oz double cream
2 to 3 Tbsp cognac or whisky

1. Prepare the pie: With an electric mixer, beat the eggs until thick and creamy, about 3 minutes. Gradually beat in the condensed milk, lime juice and rind. Pour into the tart case and refrigerate until completely set, at least 4 hours or overnight.

2. Prepare the Pineau des Charentes cream: Beat the cream, sugar and Pineau des Charentes until stiff peaks form. Spoon the cream into a decorating bag fitted with a medium star nozzle and pipe a decorative border around the pie.

3. Prepare the chocolate sauce: In a small saucepan over medium-low heat, heat the chocolate and cream until melted and smooth, stirring frequently. Remove from heat and stir in the cognac.

Country-Style Peach Tart

6–8 SERVINGS

1 quantity Basic Sweet Shortcrust Pastry (p. 26)
900 g/2 lb ripe peaches
2 to 3 Tbsp lemon juice
15 g/½ oz butter
3 to 4 Tbsp sugar
2 Tbsp plain flour
½ tsp cinnamon
4 Tbsp fresh breadcrumbs, toasted or homemade dried breadcrumbs

1. Lightly spray or oil a large baking sheet. On a lightly floured surface, roll out the pastry to a 32–35 cm/13 or 14 inch circle. Slide on to the baking sheet and refrigerate 30 minutes.

2. Peel the peaches. Cut each in half and, using a teaspoon, scoop out each stone. Cut peaches into thick slices and sprinkle with the lemon juice. Melt the butter in a large frying pan over high heat. Add the peach slices and stir-fry for 2–3 minutes until the peaches just begin to soften. Sprinkle in the sugar, flour and cinnamon and toss to coat the peach slices well. Remove from heat and cool about 5 minutes.

3. Preheat oven to 200°C/400°F/Gas Mark 6. Remove the dough from the refrigerator to soften, about 5 minutes. Sprinkle the pastry with the toasted or dried breadcrumbs and spoon the peach mixture on to the dough to within 7.5–10 cm/3–4 inches of the border.

4. Using your fingertips, fold and crimp the wide border of the dough over the fruit towards the centre. Sprinkle with a little sugar. If the pastry cracks or is uneven, just pinch it together. Bake until crisp and golden and fruit is bubbling, about 35–40 minutes. Transfer to a wire rack to cool slightly. Serve warm or at room temperature.

Southern Pecan Tart

8–10 SERVINGS

This all-American classic pie is delicious served warm with whipped cream, soured cream or vanilla ice-cream.

1 (22 cm/9 inch) tart case, lined with Basic Sweet Shortcrust Pastry (p. 26)
225 g/8 oz pecan halves
3 eggs
225 g/8 oz dark brown sugar
75 g/3 oz golden syrup
Grated rind and juice of 1/2 lemon
50 g/2 oz butter, melted
1/2 tsp vanilla essence

1. Preheat oven to 180°C/350°F/Gas Mark 4. Pick out about 75 g/3 oz of perfect pecan halves and set aside. Coarsely chop the remaining nuts.

2. Beat the eggs and sugar together in a large bowl. Beat in the golden syrup, grated lemon rind and juice, melted butter, vanilla essence and the chopped pecans. Pour mixture into the tart case and carefully place on to a baking sheet.

3. Arrange the perfect pecans in concentric circles on top of the egg-sugar mixture and bake until the filling is set and slightly puffed and pecans are well coloured, for about 40 minutes. Transfer to a wire rack to cool. Serve warm or at room temperature.

Coconut Custard Pie

6–8 SERVINGS

This is a classic pie – a sweet creamy coconut filling in a tender flaky pastry crust.

1 (22 cm/9 inch) pie plate lined with Basic Shortcrust Pastry (p. 26), baked blind
175 g/6 oz granulated sugar
4 Tbsp cornflour
1/8 tsp salt
475 ml/16 fl oz milk
175 ml/6 fl oz double cream
3 egg yolks
25 g/1 oz unsalted butter, diced
2 tsp vanilla essence
225 g/8 oz desiccated coconut
250 ml/8 fl oz double cream

1. In a medium saucepan, combine the sugar, cornflour and salt. Slowly whisk in the milk and half the cream and bring to the boil over medium heat.

2. Beat the egg yolks with the remaining cream and slowly pour into the thickened milk mixture, whisking constantly and rapidly to avoid lumps. Boil for 1 minute, whisking constantly. Remove from heat and beat in the butter, vanilla essence and 150 g/5 oz of the coconut. Pour into the tart case and smooth the top evenly. Cool, then refrigerate.

3. Preheat oven to 220°C/425°F/Gas Mark 7. Spread the remaining coconut on a baking sheet and toast until golden, stirring occasionally, about 5 minutes. Cool the coconut completely.

4. Beat the cream until soft peaks form. Spoon into a decorating bag filled with a medium star nozzle and pipe a border of cream around the edge. Alternatively spoon cream on to the tart and swirl with the back of a spoon. Sprinkle with the toasted coconut and serve cold.

CHAPTER THREE

FRUIT DESSERTS

Clementines in Rosemary-Wine Sauce

8 SERVINGS

This pretty, refreshing dessert gets its unusual tang from the rosemary-scented syrup. Small tangerines or oranges can be used instead of the clementines.

ROSEMARY-WINE SYRUP

1 bottle fruity white wine
225 g/8 oz granulated sugar
2 to 3 sprigs fresh rosemary
2 cardamom pods, lightly crushed
1 cinnamon stick
2 cloves
1 bay leaf

8 clementines or tangerines

1. Put the wine and remaining ingredients, except the clementines or tangerines, in a large, heavy-based saucepan. Bring to the boil, stirring occasionally to dissolve the sugar. Reduce the heat and simmer, about 20 minutes.

2. Remove the orange zest in wide strips from two clementines and add to the simmering syrup. With a sharp knife, peel all the clementines or tangerines, removing the white pith.

3. Lower the peeled fruits into the syrup and simmer for about 10 minutes, stirring gently from time to time to be sure they are well coated. Remove from heat and cool to room temperature. Transfer to a serving bowl and chill the clementines in their syrup 5–6 hours or overnight. Spoon the fruit into shallow bowls, ladle over some of the syrup and serve.

TIP: The clementines or tangerines can be prepared up to three days ahead.

Baked Pears in Ginger Cream

4 SERVINGS

This is a simple but delicious dessert. The pears absorb the cream and have a buttery texture and sweet ginger flavour.

400 g/14 oz granulated sugar
350 ml/12 fl oz water
2.5 cm/1 inch piece fresh ginger, peeled and thinly sliced
4 large pears
350 ml/12 fl oz double cream
1 tsp vanilla essence
1 tsp ground ginger
1/4 tsp cinnamon
1 Tbsp finely chopped preserved fresh ginger
1 Tbsp ginger syrup

1. Put 350 g/12 oz of sugar in a large saucepan with the water and the sliced ginger. Bring to the boil over medium-high heat, stirring to dissolve the sugar, then reduce to a simmer.

2. Peel the pears. Cut in half lengthways and remove the cores. Lower each pear half into the simmering syrup and poach until just tender, about 10 minutes.

3. Preheat oven to 180°C/350°F/Gas Mark 4. In a bowl, whisk the cream with the remaining 50 g/2 oz sugar, vanilla, ground ginger, cinnamon, chopped fresh ginger and the ginger syrup.

4. Butter an oven-proof baking dish large enough to hold the pears in a single layer, and arrange the pears, cut-sides down, in the dish. Slowly spoon over the cream mixture, allowing it to seep down between the pears.

5. Bake about 40 minutes, basting the pears with the cream for the first 20 minutes, until the pears are tender when pierced with a knife and the cream is thickened and bubbling. Cool before serving.

Summer Pudding

6 SERVINGS

This is a classic English summer dessert. The lightly sweetened berries are enclosed in a layer of bread which soaks up the fruit juices. Begin at least one day ahead. Serve with additional raspberry sauce and whipped cream.

Raspberry Sauce (page 46)

PUDDING

225 g/8 oz strawberries, cut in half
225 g/8 oz raspberries
225 g/8 oz blackberries
225 g/8 oz redcurrants or blueberries
100 g/4 oz caster sugar
50 ml/2 fl oz orange juice or water
8 to 10 slices day-old, dense white bread

Extra berries for decoration
Whipped cream for serving

1. Prepare the raspberry sauce and chill until ready to serve. Prepare the pudding: Put the fruit in a large saucepan with the sugar and juice or water. Set over medium-low heat and stir occasionally until sugar dissolves and the juices begin to run. Remove from heat and turn the fruit into a colander or large strainer set over a bowl to catch the juices.

2. Lightly oil a 1½ l/2½ pt bowl or basin. Trim the crusts of bread and discard. Cut each bread slice into halves or triangles. Quickly dip each slice of bread into the fruit juices and arrange the pieces juice-side out, over the base and side of the bowl to line completely. Cut any leftover pieces to fill in any gaps, so there are no spaces; trim even with the top edge of the bowl. Reserve enough slices to cover the top.

3. Spoon the fruit into the bread-lined bowl or basin and pour over any remaining fruit juices. Cover with the reserved bread pieces and any trimmings. Cover with cling film and use a small plate or saucer which

just fits on top of the bowl, to sit on top of the pudding. Weight the plate with one or two heavy tins and refrigerate overnight.

4. To turn out, remove the weights, plate and cling film. Run a knife blade around the edge of the pudding to separate it from the bowl and invert the pudding on to a serving plate. Holding the plate and bowl tightly together, give a firm shake to release the pudding. Carefully lift off the bowl or basin. Sprinkle a few berries over the top of the pudding and around the base. Serve with whipped cream and the raspberry sauce.

Fruity Champagne Jelly with Summer Berries

8–10 SERVINGS

This refreshing delicate dessert is perfect for a summer party. Use a variety of berries in season and, if you like, substitute a dry white wine for the champagne. If you prefer, serve with a raspberry or other fruit sauce.

450 g/1 lb granulated sugar
1 bottle dry champagne or other sparkling dry white wine
2 Tbsp unflavoured gelatine
150 g/5 oz ripe strawberries, cut in halves or quarters
150 g/5 oz raspberries
150 g/5 oz blueberries
150 g/5 oz small strawberries or blackberries

1. Put the sugar and champagne or wine into a medium saucepan and bring to a boil over medium-high heat, stirring to completely dissolve the sugar. Remove from heat.

2. Meanwhile, sprinkle the gelatine over cold water and allow to stand until translucent and spongy, about 5 minutes. Do not stir. Stand the bowl in a small saucepan with just simmering water and heat gently until just melted. When gelatine is completely melted, stir gently, then gradually stir into the champagne mixture.

3. Put the berries in a large bowl and pour the champagne-gelatine mixture over them. Set aside and allow to cool, but do not allow to set. Rinse a 900 g/2 lb loaf tin with cold water and spoon in half the liquid and fruits. Refrigerate until set; keep the remaining mixture at room temperature. When the first layer is set, carefully spoon over the remaining fruits and liquid; refrigerate until set, 4–6 hours or overnight. Cover the loaf tin tightly with cling film.

4. To turn out, dip the bottom half of the tin into warm water for 2–3 seconds; wipe dry. Run a sharp knife around the edge to break the air lock. Place a serving dish over the tin and, holding them tightly together, invert them quickly with a firm shake; the dessert should drop on to the plate. If not, rest a hot cloth on the bottom of the inverted tin for 2–3 seconds and try again. Carefully lift off the tin, wipe any drips, and refrigerate to reset the surface.

5. To serve, dip a thin-bladed knife into hot water, wipe dry. Cut into slices and if you like, serve with a raspberry or other fruit sauce.

TIP: To melt gelatine in the microwave: Soften as above, then microwave on High (100% power) at 10–15 second intervals until completely melted; stir. (Do not allow to boil rapidly as this will inhibit its setting properties.)

Vanilla Poached Pears
with Vanilla Custard

6 SERVINGS

The flavour of real vanilla is exquisite and goes well with the tender pears and the custard.

VANILLA POACHED PEARS
175 g/6 oz granulated sugar
1 vanilla pod
475 ml/16 fl oz water
6 ripe pears
lemon juice

VANILLA POD CUSTARD SAUCE
1 vanilla pod
600 ml/1 pt milk
9 egg yolks
50 g/2 oz caster sugar

Slivered toasted almonds or hazelnuts, for decoration (optional)

1. Put the sugar in a large saucepan. Split the vanilla pod lengthways with a sharp knife, scrape the seeds into the saucepan and add the split pod. Add the water and cook until the sugar has dissolved.

2. Peel the pears, rubbing each with a little lemon juice. Core each pear from the bottom, leaving the stem end intact. Cut a thin slice from the bottom of each pear to make a flat bottom. Lower into the sugar syrup and add enough water to cover.

3. Cut out a circle of greaseproof paper and cover the top of the pears; cover the saucepan. Simmer for 20 minutes until tender. Remove from heat and cool the pears in the syrup.

4. Remove the pears to a large serving bowl with a slotted spoon. Bring the syrup to the boil. Boil rapidly for about 10 minutes to reduce by about half. Strain over the reserved pears and cool completely. Cover and refrigerate for several hours or overnight.

5. Prepare the custard: Split the vanilla pod as in step 1 and bring to the boil in a medium heavy-based saucepan with the milk. Beat the egg yolks with the caster sugar until pale and thick. Pour the hot milk over the egg yolk mixture, whisking constantly. Return to the saucepan and cook over low heat until the sauce thickens and coats the back of a wooden spoon, stirring constantly. (Do not boil or the sauce will curdle.) Strain into a bowl and cool completely. Cover and refrigerate.

6. Serve each pear with some of its syrup. Spoon some custard over each and sprinkle with a few toasted slivered almonds or hazelnuts.

Apricot-Glazed Berries
with Mascarpone Cream

6–8 SERVINGS

Summer berries make an ideal summer fruit dessert. Keep them simple with this easy glaze and serve with a luscious mascarpone cream.

MASCARPONE CREAM
250 g/9 oz mascarpone (Italian cream cheese), at room temperature*
120 ml/4 fl oz double cream
2 tsp caster sugar
2 Tbsp cognac or orange-flavoured liqueur
1 tsp vanilla essence
2 egg whites

GLAZED BERRIES
675 g/1½ lb mixed fresh berries such as strawberries (halved if large), raspberries, blackberries and blueberries
3 Tbsp soft brown sugar
3 Tbsp apricot jam
85 ml/3 fl oz cognac or orange-flavoured liqueur
50 g/2 oz toasted slivered almonds or hazelnuts

1. Prepare the mascarpone cream: With an electric mixer, beat the mascarpone, cream and sugar until smooth and well blended, 1–2 minutes. Beat in the cognac or orange-flavoured liqueur and vanilla. In another bowl with cleaned beaters, beat the egg whites until soft peaks form; beat 30 seconds longer. Stir a spoonful of egg whites into the cream mixture to lighten it, then fold in the remaining egg whites until just blended. Spoon into a serving bowl and refrigerate, covered, until ready to serve.

2. Put the berries in a large serving bowl and toss lightly to mix; set aside. Put the brown sugar, apricot jam and cognac or orange-flavoured liqueur in a small saucepan and bring to the boil over medium heat, stirring to blend. Slowly drizzle the glaze over the berries and sprinkle with the toasted almonds or hazelnuts. Allow to stand at room temperature for at least 1 hour before serving with the cream.

*Mascarpone is an Italian cream cheese available in large supermarkets and delicatessens.

**This dessert contains uncooked egg whites.

Caramelized Apple Charlotte

with Lemon Crème Anglaise

6 SERVINGS

This is a classic dessert. A tangy apple purée is encased in a buttery bread crust which caramelizes as it bakes. The Lemon Crème Anglaise makes a perfect accompaniment.

CREME ANGLAISE

600 ml/1 pt milk
1 large lemon
8 egg yolks
50 g/2 oz granulated sugar

APPLE CHARLOTTE

1 kg/2½ lb sharp-flavoured dessert apples
2 Tbsp water
2 Tbsp lemon juice
175 g/6 oz soft brown sugar
1 tsp cinnamon
½ tsp freshly ground nutmeg
75 g/3 oz unsalted butter, melted
Granulated sugar for sprinkling
7 to 8 slices dense white bread

1. Put the milk in a heavy-based medium saucepan. Remove the peel from the lemon in wide strips, add to the milk in the pan and bring to the boil.

2. With an electric mixer, beat the egg yolks and sugar until thick, about 3 minutes. Whisk in the hot milk and return the mixture to the saucepan. Cook the sauce until it begins to thicken and coats the back of a wooden spoon, stirring constantly. (Do not allow it to boil or it will curdle.) Strain into a chilled bowl, cool and refrigerate.

3. Peel the apples. Quarter, core and cut into thick slices. Put the apple slices, water and lemon juice in a frying pan and cook for about 15 minutes until the apples are very soft. Add the sugar, cinnamon and nutmeg and cook until the apples are almost puréed and all the liquid has evaporated.

4. Preheat oven to 200°C/400°F/Gas Mark 6. Brush a 1.4 l/2½ pt charlotte mould or soufflé dish with a little melted butter and line the bottom with nonstick baking paper. Butter again and sprinkle with sugar. Trim the crusts from the bread slices and brush one side with the butter. Cut two of the bread slices into triangles and line the base of the dish, buttered-side down. Use more bread to line the sides of the dish, buttered-side out, leaving no gaps.

5. Spoon in the apple purée and cover the top with any remaining bread slices, buttered-side up.

6. Bake 20 minutes; reduce oven temperature to 180°C/350°F/Gas Mark 4 and bake 25 minutes until browned and crisp. Turn out and serve with the custard.

Peach Melba

6 SERVINGS

The great French chef August Escoffier created this now famous dessert for the opera singer Dame Nellie Melba. It's a wonderful combination of poached peaches, vanilla ice-cream and raspberry sauce.

POACHED PEACHES

50 g/2 oz sugar
1 vanilla pod, split lengthways
2 to 3 strips orange peel
Juice of 1 orange
900 ml/1½ pt water
3 large ripe peaches

RASPBERRY SAUCE

450 g/1 lb fresh or frozen raspberries
1 Tbsp lemon juice
2 to 3 Tbsp sugar
2 Tbsp raspberry-flavoured liqueur (optional)
Vanilla ice-cream for serving

1. Put the sugar in a large saucepan, with the split vanilla pod, orange peel strips, orange juice and the water. Bring to the boil, stirring occasionally until the sugar dissolves.

2. Cut peaches in half lengthways and remove stones. Lower peaches into poaching syrup, cut-side down, and press a piece of greaseproof paper against surface. Cover and simmer 12–15 minutes, until tender. Cool in the syrup.

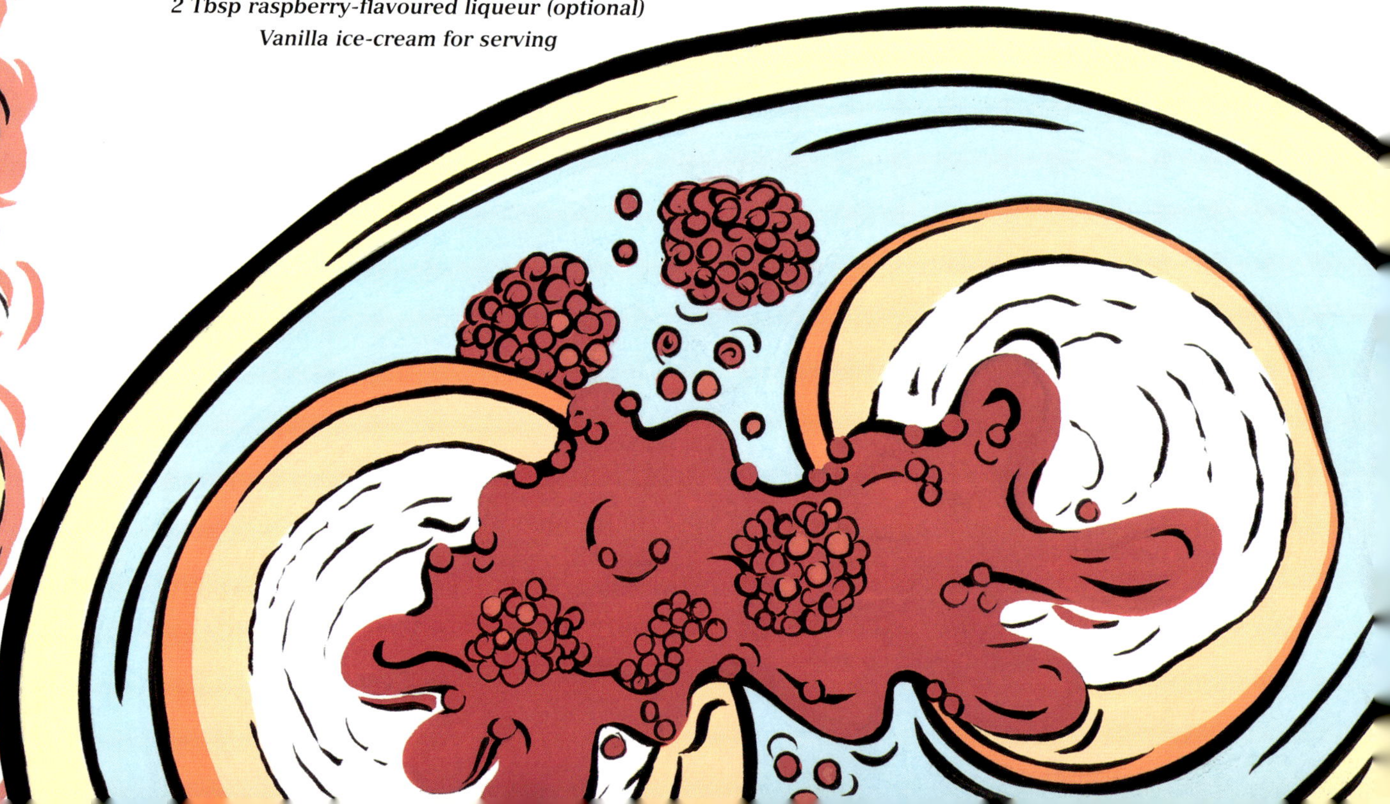

3. Remove peaches from their syrup and peel off skins. Drain on kitchen paper (reserve the syrup for another use). Cover and refrigerate for several hours or overnight.

4. Prepare the raspberry sauce: Place raspberries, lemon juice and sugar in a food processor fitted with a metal blade. Process 1 minute. Press through a fine sieve into a small bowl, stir in the raspberry liqueur and refrigerate 1–2 hours until well chilled.

5. To serve, place a peach half, cut-side up on a dessert plate, fill with a scoop of vanilla ice-cream and spoon the raspberry sauce over the ice-cream.

Tropical Fruit Salad with Thai-Scented Coconut Cream

6 SERVINGS

If fresh coconut milk is unavailable, use a 400 g/13½ oz tin of coconut milk diluted with 175 ml/6 fl oz water.

COCONUT MILK

1 large heavy coconut
475 ml/16 fl oz boiling water

THAI-SCENTED COCONUT CREAM

3 Tbsp granulated sugar
50 ml/2 fl oz tinned cream of coconut
6 cardamom pods, lightly crushed
2 stalks fresh lemon grass, trimmed and bruised*
5 cm/2 inch piece fresh ginger, peeled and sliced
*2 star anise**
1 vanilla pod, split lengthways

675 g/1½ lb chopped tropical fruits, such as mango, papaya, melon, peach, banana, kiwi, peeled lychees and star fruit
75 g/3 oz fresh raspberries
Mint sprigs for decoration (optional)

1. Using a screwdriver, pierce the three "eyes" of the coconut and drain the liquid into a bowl. (Reserve for another use.) Put the coconut in a heavy-duty freezer bag and twist lightly to close. Using a hammer or back of a meat cleaver, strike the coconut to break the shell in several places. Remove pieces from the bag and, using a small sharp knife, separate the flesh from the "hairy" brown shell. Remove the brown skin with a vegetable peeler or small sharp knife. Cut the coconut flesh into small pieces.

2. Fit a food processor with a fine shredding disc and with the machine running drop the pieces through the feed tube to shred. Turn the shredded coconut into a bowl. Put the shredded coconut into the processor and with the machine running, pour the boiling water through the feed tube; process about 30 seconds. Pour back into the bowl and allow to cool until just warm.

3. In small batches, press the coconut mixture through a fine sieve set over a large mixing bowl; press very hard extracting as much liquid as possible; this is the coconut milk. You should be able to extract about 475 ml/16 fl oz.

4. Put the coconut milk, sugar, cream of coconut, cardamom pods, lemon grass, ginger, star anise and vanilla pod in a large saucepan and bring to a simmer. Cool completely, then refrigerate overnight. Strain into a large measuring cup or jug and discard the spices.

5. To serve, arrange the fruit in a large shallow serving bowl. Pour over the chilled coconut cream, sprinkle with the raspberries and decorate with fresh mint sprigs.

**Lemon grass* can be found in large supermarkets or Oriental grocers. *Star anise* is available in large supermarkets or Chinese specialist grocers.

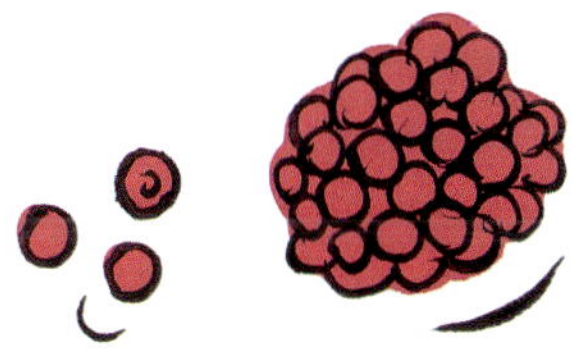

Fresh Strawberries
with Grand Marnier Sabayon

4 SERVINGS

A sabayon is like a hot mousse made with flavoured sweetened egg yolks which are lightly cooked. This sauce is delicious over any fruit.

GRAND MARNIER SABAYON

3 egg yolks
2 Tbsp caster sugar
120 ml/4 fl oz white wine
3 Tbsp Grand Marnier or other orange-flavoured liqueur

STRAWBERRIES

675 g/1½ lb fresh strawberries
1 tsp lemon juice
1 Tbsp Grand Marnier or other orange-flavoured liqueur
Icing sugar for dusting, sifted

Toasted, slivered almonds for decoration

1. Prepare the sabayon: Put the egg yolks, sugar, wine and liqueur into the top of a double boiler or heatproof bowl and whisk to blend. Set the top of the double boiler or heatproof bowl over the bottom half of saucepan of simmering water. With an electric mixer, over the heat, beat until the mixture thickens and lightens in colour and the beaters leave a trail on the bottom of the bowl, about 10 minutes. Remove from heat and continue beating until mixture cools slightly. Set aside, but keep warm.

2. Prepare the strawberries: Hull the berries and brush clean (try not to wash). Slice each berry lengthways and, in a bowl, toss with the lemon juice and liqueur. Dust with icing sugar.

3. Arrange the strawberries in individual serving dishes and spoon over the sabayon. Sprinkle with toasted slivered almonds and serve immediately.

Peaches and Cream Meringues

8 SERVINGS

The crunchy meringues are filled with mascarpone, whipped cream and lightly poached peaches – an elegant combination for any special occasion.

POACHED PEACHES

100 g/4 oz sugar
½ cinnamon stick
2 strips lemon peel
750 ml/1¼ pt water
4 ripe peaches

MERINGUES

3 egg whites
¼ tsp cream of tartar
175 g/6 oz caster sugar
1 tsp vanilla essence

MASCARPONE CREAM

300 ml/½ pt double cream
2 Tbsp Amaretto liqueur
100 g/4 oz mascarpone
50 g/2 oz caster sugar

Toasted pine nuts for decoration

1. Put the sugar, cinnamon stick, lemon peel and water into a saucepan large enough to hold the peaches. Bring to the boil, stirring until sugar dissolves. Lower the peaches into the syrup. Simmer for 10 minutes. Cool in the syrup.

2. Remove peaches from the syrup and skin. Cut each peach in half and remove the stone. Slice the halves and put into a bowl. Bring the syrup back to a boil and boil rapidly until reduced and syrupy, about 10 minutes. Strain over the peach slices and cool. Refrigerate.

3. Preheat oven to 150°C/275°F/Gas Mark 1. Line a large baking sheet with nonstick baking paper. Beat the egg whites until frothy. Add the cream of tartar and beat until stiff peaks just begin to form. Gradually sprinkle over about three-quarters of the sugar, beating well after each addition until stiff and glossy. Fold in the remaining sugar and vanilla essence.

4. Spoon the mixture into eight small circles on to the baking sheet, making a well in the centre of each.

5. Bake about 40 minutes until set. Turn off the oven and leave in the oven 45 minutes longer to dry out. Remove meringues to a wire rack to cool.

6. Prepare the mascarpone cream: Beat the cream with the Amaretto until soft peaks form. Beat the mascarpone with the sugar until smooth. Beat a spoonful of cream into the mascarpone mixture to lighten it, then fold in the remaining cream.

7. Fill each meringue with a spoonful of the cream. Arrange the peach slices on top, spooning a little extra syrup around the meringue. Sprinkle with a few toasted pine nuts.

Sautéed Bananas with Caribbean Rum Sauce

4 SERVINGS

This is a fantastic combination of bananas with those Caribbean flavours that go so well together – lime, pineapple, brown sugar and rum; especially delicious with coconut or vanilla ice-cream.

CARIBBEAN RUM SAUCE

100 g/4 oz granulated sugar
100 g/4 oz dark brown sugar
85 ml/3 fl oz water
450 g/1 lb tin crushed pineapple with its own juice
Grated rind and juice of 1 lime
45 g/1½ oz unsalted butter
2 Tbsp dark rum

25 g/1 oz unsalted butter
4 bananas
4 kumquats, thinly sliced (optional)
50 ml/2 fl oz dark rum

Vanilla or coconut ice-cream for serving
Mint sprigs for decoration

1. Prepare the sauce: Put all the ingredients for the sauce except the rum in a medium saucepan and bring to the boil over medium heat, stirring frequently to dissolve the sugar. Simmer gently until reduced and thickened, about 7 minutes. Remove from heat, stir in the rum and keep warm.

2. In a large frying pan, melt the butter over medium-high heat. Peel the bananas and cut in half lengthways. When the butter has stopped bubbling and is very hot, add the bananas. Cook about 5 minutes, turning once halfway through cooking, until soft and just tender. Sprinkle over the kumquats if using and carefully pour in the rum. With a long match and tilting the pan, ignite the rum. Shake the pan to distribute the rum and remove from heat.

3. Scoop the vanilla or coconut ice-cream into four large dessert dishes. Divide the banana mixture evenly around the ice-cream and spoon over the warm Caribbean rum sauce. Decorate each serving with a few sprigs of mint.

TIP: The sauce can be made up to three days ahead, then gently reheated before serving.

CHAPTER FOUR

FROZEN DESSERTS

Chocolate Marquise
with Espresso Crème Anglaise

8–10 SERVINGS

MARQUISE

225 g/8 oz good-quality plain or bittersweet chocolate, chopped
65 g/2½ oz unsalted butter, softened
4 large eggs, separated
2 Tbsp cognac or dark rum
¼ tsp cream of tartar

ESPRESSO CREME ANGLAISE

600 ml/1 pt milk
1½ Tbsp instant espresso coffee powder, dissolved in 2 Tbsp hot water
9 egg yolks
50 g/2 oz granulated sugar
1 to 2 Tbsp coffee-flavoured liqueur (optional)
1 tsp vanilla essence

1. Line a 1.2 l/2 pt terrine or 20 x 10 cm/8 x 4 inch loaf tin with cling film, smoothing out as many wrinkles as possible.

2. Heat the chocolate and butter until melted. Remove from heat and beat in yolks, one at a time; add the cognac.

3. Beat the egg whites until frothy. Add the cream of tartar and beat until the whites form soft peaks, beat 30 seconds longer. Fold the whites into the chocolate mixture. Spoon into the terrine smoothing the top. Cover and freeze overnight.

4. Prepare the sauce: Bring the milk to the boil with the coffee mixture. Beat egg yolks and sugar until thick and creamy, 2–3 minutes. Whisk in the hot milk and return to the heat. Cook until thickened. (Do not boil or it will curdle.) Strain and stir in the coffee liqueur, if using and vanilla. Cool then refrigerate.

5. Invert the marquise on to a serving dish. Remove the cling film. Serve in thin slices with a little espresso crème anglaise.

Nectarine and Mango Ice-Cream

6–8 SERVINGS

250 ml/8 fl oz water
225 g/8 oz granulated sugar, plus 2 to 3 Tbsp
1 vanilla pod, split in half lengthways
5 ripe nectarines
1 large ripe mango
Juice of 3 ripe passionfruit or 1 orange, strained
475 ml/16 fl oz double cream

1. Put the water and 225 g/8 oz sugar in a saucepan. Scrape the seeds from the vanilla pod into the saucepan. Bring to the boil over medium-high heat, stirring to dissolve the sugar. Score the bottom of each nectarine and lower into the syrup. Simmer gently, 10 minutes, until very tender (the time will depend on the ripeness of the fruit). Remove from heat and cool.

2. Peel the mango. Cut down both sides of the centre stone to remove as much flesh as possible; cut into pieces. Scrape off any flesh still attached to the stone. Set aside.

3. Remove the nectarines from the syrup and remove and discard the skins. Cut each nectarine in half and remove the stone. Put the nectarine halves in a food processor. Add 350 ml/12 fl oz of the syrup, the mango pieces and the passionfruit or orange juice and process until a smooth purée forms. Remove 175 ml/6 fl oz of purée. Taste for sweetness and add more sugar if necessary. Chill until ready to serve. Add the cream and 2 to 3 tablespoons of sugar to the processor and blend. Taste and add more sugar if necessary.

4. Pour the mixture into an ice-cream maker and freeze as the manufacturer directs. Transfer to a freezerproof container and freeze 3–4 hours until firm. Serve with the fruit purée.

Bitter Chocolate Sorbet
with Tangerine Sauce

6–8 SERVINGS

SORBET

225 g/8 oz sugar
475 ml/16 fl oz water
150 g/5 oz unsweetened chocolate, chopped
100 g/4 oz good-quality plain chocolate, chopped

TANGERINE SAUCE

Segments of 2 tangerines
Grated rind of 2 tangerines
350 ml/12 fl oz freshly squeezed tangerine juice
50 g/2 oz sugar or to taste
2 tsp cornflour dissolved in 2 tsp cold water

1. Prepare the sorbet: Put the sugar and water in a saucepan and bring to the boil over medium-high heat, stirring to dissolve the sugar. Boil for 2 minutes.

2. Put the chocolate in a food processor. Process for 30 seconds until finely chopped.

3. With the machine running, pour the boiling syrup over the chocolate. Allow the machine to continue running 1–2 minutes until chocolate is completely melted and mixture is smooth.

4. Strain the chocolate mixture into a large measuring jug and cool completely, then refrigerate until chilled, stirring occasionally. Transfer to an ice-cream maker and freeze as the manufacturer directs. Spoon into a container and freeze 2 hours or overnight.

5. Prepare the sauce: Put the tangerine segments in a bowl and set aside. Bring the tangerine rind, juice and sugar to the boil over medium-high heat; boil 2 minutes. Whisk the cornflour into the boiling juice mixture until thickened, simmer 1 minute. Pour into the bowl with tangerine segments. Cool, stirring from time to time. Chill.

6. Soften the sorbet for 10 minutes. Spoon a little tangerine sauce over each serving.

Celebration Brownie-Baked Alaska

12–14 SERVINGS

This spectacular-looking dessert is ideal for a party, as it can be prepared well ahead of time and baked just before serving. Any combination of ice-cream flavours can be used, but the ones below work beautifully.

BROWNIE LAYER

100 g/4 oz unsalted butter
50 g/2 oz unsweetened chocolate, chopped
225 g/8 oz granulated sugar
2 eggs
1 tsp vanilla essence
50 g/2 oz plain flour
50 g/2 oz pecans, chopped and toasted

FILLING

475 ml/16 fl oz Rich Chocolate Ice-Cream (p.57) or other good-quality chocolate ice-cream
475 ml/16 fl oz good-quality vanilla ice-cream
475 ml/16 fl oz good-quality raspberry sorbet

MERINGUE TOPPING

4 egg whites

1/4 tsp cream of tartar

225 g/8 oz sugar

2 tsp vanilla essence

Fresh raspberry sauce (p. 46) to serve (optional)

1. Preheat oven to 180°C/350°F/Gas Mark 4. Lightly grease a 20 cm/8 inch cake tin. Line the bottom with nonstick baking paper or greaseproof paper; regrease and dust lightly with flour.

2. Melt the butter and chocolate. Stir in the sugar, eggs and vanilla essence. Stir in the flour and pecans. Spoon into the tin.

3. Bake about 25 minutes. Remove to a wire rack to cool briefly, then invert on to the rack to cool completely. Wrap tightly until ready for use.

4. Line a 1.5–2 l/2½–3 pt freezer-proof mixing bowl with a diameter of not more than 20 cm/8 inches with cling film, allowing enough film to fold over bottom when filled. Freeze while softening the chocolate ice-cream, about 20 minutes.

5. Spread the softened chocolate ice-cream with an even 2.5 cm/1 inch layer around the bowl to within about 1 cm/½ inch of top edge of bowl. Cover and freeze 30 minutes. Soften the white chocolate ice-cream, about 20 minutes.

6. Remove the bowl from the freezer. Spread the softened white chocolate ice-cream against the chocolate layer about 2.5 cm/1 inch thick. Cover, then refreeze about 30 minutes. Soften the sorbet.

7. Fill the centre of the bowl with the raspberry sorbet. Place the brownie layer on to the surface of the ice-cream filled bowl pressing firmly against the surface; trim to fit if necessary. Fold the excess cling film over the top of bowl and freeze overnight.

8. Prepare the topping: Preheat oven to 240°C/450°F/Gas Mark 8. Beat the egg whites and cream of tartar until stiff peaks form. Gradually add the sugar, 2 tablespoons at a time, beating well after each addition, until stiff and glossy. Beat in the vanilla. Spoon into a large decorating bag fitted with a medium star nozzle.

9. Remove the ice-cream filled bowl from the freezer and peel back the cling film. Invert the bowl on to a heatproof serving dish and remove remaining cling film. Starting at the centre of the top, pipe vertical stripes of rosettes or scrolls with edges touching, around side of dessert. Pipe a border around the bottom edge to seal completely. (The dessert can be frozen at this stage for several hours.) Bake 3–5 minutes until golden and set.

Caramel Crunch Ice-Cream in Biscuit Cups

6–8 SERVINGS

CARAMEL CRUNCH ICE-CREAM

45 g/1½ oz blanched almonds
225 g/8 oz granulated sugar
50 ml/2 fl oz water
475 ml/16 fl oz milk
6 eggs yolks
250 ml/8 fl oz double cream

BISCUIT CUPS

45 g/1½ oz whole blanched almonds, lightly toasted
45 g/1½ oz caster sugar
45 g/1½ oz unsalted butter, softened
2 egg whites
½ tsp almond essence
25 g/1 oz plain flour, sifted

CARAMEL SAUCE

250 g/9 oz granulated sugar
300 g/10 oz cups water

1. Prepare the ice-cream: Lightly oil a baking sheet. Place the almonds in a saucepan with 75 g/3 oz of sugar, sprinkle with the water and bring to the boil. Boil without stirring for 4–5 minutes until syrup is a caramel colour and nuts begin to pop. Immediately pour out on to the baking sheet. Do not touch – caramel is dangerously hot. Cool completely.

2. Break the mixture into pieces and place in a food processor. Process to fine crumbs.

3. Bring the milk to the boil. Beat the egg yolks and remaining sugar 2–3 minutes until thick. Whisk the hot milk into the egg mixture and cook about 3–4 minutes until the mixture thickens and coats the back of the spoon.

4. Strain and cool. Refrigerate until chilled, then stir in the cream and caramel-nut mixture. Transfer to an ice-cream maker and freeze as manufacturer directs. Spoon into a container and freeze overnight.

5. Prepare the biscuit cups: Preheat oven to 200°C/400°F/Gas Mark 6. Butter two baking sheets. Process the almonds and 2 tablespoons of the sugar until fine crumbs form. Beat the butter until creamy. Add remaining sugar and beat 1 minute until fluffy. Gradually beat in the egg whites and almond essence. Sift the flour over the butter mixture and fold in, then fold in almond-sugar mixture.

6. Drop the mixture by tablespoons 20 cm/8 inches apart on to prepared baking sheets. With the back of a wet spoon, spread each mound into a thin 10 cm/4 inch round.

7. Bake one sheet at a time, about 4–5 minutes. Remove to a wire rack and, quickly transfer each to an upturned drinking glass, pressing over the bottom to form a fluted basket. Allow to set; continue with remaining batter.

8. Prepare the caramel sauce: Cook the sugar and half the water. Boil without stirring 4–5 minutes until a golden caramel colour. Remove from heat and, standing back from pan, pour in remaining water. Cook 1–2 minutes until caramel dissolves. Cool (do not refrigerate).

9. Soften the ice-cream 15–20 minutes then fill each cup. Drizzle with a little caramel sauce.

Frozen Peanut Butter Fudge Torte

10–12 SERVINGS

Chocolate and peanut butter is a well-loved combination. It works especially well in this rich summer dessert.

PEANUT-CHOCOLATE CRUMB CRUST

225 g/8 oz chocolate wafers (about 24–26)
45 g/1½ oz dry roasted peanuts, finely chopped and toasted
50 g/2 oz unsalted butter, melted

FUDGE FILLING

120 ml/4 fl oz double cream
3 Tbsp golden syrup
150 g/5 oz plain chocolate, chopped
1 Tbsp vanilla essence

ICE-CREAM LAYER

1.5 l/2½ pt good-quality chocolate ice-cream or Rich Chocolate Ice-Cream (p. 57)
50 g/2 oz dry roasted peanuts, chopped and toasted
450 g/1 lb smooth peanut butter
250 g/9 oz honey
250 ml/8 fl oz double cream
50 g/2 oz caster sugar
1 tsp vanilla essence

1. Prepare the crumb crust: Lightly spray or oil a 22 cm/9 inch springform tin. Put the chocolate wafers and peanuts in a food processor and process to fine crumbs. Pour in the butter and process until blended. Pat on to the bottom and up sides of the tin.

2. Prepare the filling: Bring the cream and golden syrup to the boil. Remove from heat and add the chocolate, stirring until melted and smooth. Stir in the vanilla essence; set aside until cooled, stirring occasionally. Pour into the crumb-lined tin. Cool completely.

3. Soften the ice-cream 15–20 minutes until spreadable. Put the chopped nuts, peanut butter and honey in a bowl and stir. Add the ice-cream scoop by scoop and, with an electric mixer on low speed, beat in the ice-cream. Do not allow the ice-cream to melt completely. Spoon on to the fudge layer and smooth the top. Freeze 4–6 hours or overnight.

4. To assemble: Soften 5 minutes at room temperature. Run a knife around the edge of the tin to loosen, then remove the side of the tin. With an electric mixer, beat the cream with the sugar and vanilla until stiff peaks form. Spoon into a medium decorating bag fitted with a medium star nozzle and pipe cream in a lattice or other design across the top of the torte and around the edge. Serve immediately or freeze until ready to serve. Soften 5–10 minutes at room temperature before serving.

Pink Grapefruit and Campari Granita

6–8 SERVINGS

A granita is a kind of sorbet with a coarse, grainy texture. It makes an ideal dessert after a rich meal or a super refresher at a summer barbecue or outdoor meal.

100 g/4 oz granulated sugar
120 ml/4 fl oz water
750 ml/1¼ pt pink grapefruit juice, strained
120 ml/4 fl oz Campari
Fresh pink grapefruit sections for serving

1. Put the sugar and water into a medium saucepan and bring to the boil over medium-high heat, stirring frequently until sugar dissolves. Boil for 3 minutes, remove from heat and cool. Stir in grapefruit juice and Campari and pour into a 32.5 x 22 x 2.5 cm/13 x 9 x 1 inch baking dish or shallow plastic container.

2. Place the dish or container in the freezer and freeze until partially frozen, about 2 hours. Stir in the mixture occasionally bringing the frozen crystals from the edge into the centre. Freeze overnight (at least 6–8 hours).

3. To serve: Using the tines of a fork, scrape the mixture into large flakes and spoon into chilled glasses. Top with a few pink grapefruit sections and serve immediately.

Frozen Chocolate-Coated Banana Pops

MAKES 6

These chocolate-coated bananas-on-a-stick are popular with adults and children alike.

3 ripe bananas
225 g/8 oz plain chocolate, chopped
45 g/1½ oz vegetable margarine
45 g/1½ oz unsalted peanuts, finely chopped

1. Line a small baking sheet with greaseproof paper. Peel bananas, being sure to remove all stringy fibres. Cut each banana in half crossways, then insert a wooden lolly stick 3 cm/1½ inches into the cut end of each banana half. Place on a lined baking sheet and freeze 3 hours or overnight until very firm.

2. Melt the chocolate with the vegetable margarine, stirring frequently, until smooth. Pour into a tall mug or paper cup or other narrow container. Leave to cool 10–15 minutes, until thickened slightly.

3. Spread peanuts on to a small flat plate or sheet of foil. Hold the banana by the stick and dip into the melted chocolate, tilting the mug or cup and twisting until completely coated in chocolate. Quickly pull out banana and hold upright, then immediately roll in chopped nuts just until lightly coated.

4. Place on greaseproof paper-lined baking sheet and freeze until firm. Continue coating each pop and place each on the prepared baking sheet as soon as they are coated. Freeze at least 1 hour until chocolate is hardened. (Store pops covered in the freezer one to two weeks.)

TIP: Do not use metal sticks or small pointed wooden skewers as they could be harmful or cause injury to small children.

Rum-Raisin Surprise Bombe

10 SERVINGS

A rich frozen dessert, you can make this for an extra-special occasion.

DOUBLE CHOCOLATE RUM-RAISIN ICE-CREAM

65 g/2½ oz raisins
50 ml/2 fl oz plus 1 Tbsp light rum
150 g/5 oz good-quality white chocolate, chopped
25 g/1 oz unsweetened chocolate, chopped
325 ml/11 fl oz milk
3 egg yolks
2 Tbsp granulated sugar
75 g/3 oz honey
250 ml/8 fl oz double cream

WHITE CHOCOLATE MOUSSE

65 g/2½ oz sultanas
50 ml/2 fl oz plus 1 Tbsp light rum
250 ml/8 fl oz double cream
150 g/5 oz good-quality white chocolate, chopped
2 egg whites
¼ tsp cream of tartar
50 g/2 oz caster sugar

WHITE CHOCOLATE-RUM SAUCE

175 g/6 oz good-quality white chocolate
175 ml/6 fl oz double cream
½ tsp cinnamon
15 g/½ oz unsalted butter, softened
2 to 4 Tbsp dark or light rum

1. Prepare the ice-cream: Soak the raisins in 50 ml/2 fl oz rum for 2 hours.

2. Heat the white chocolate and unsweetened chocolate with 85 ml/3 fl oz milk until melted.

3. Bring the remaining milk to the boil. With an electric mixer, beat the egg yolks with the sugar and honey until thickened. Whisk the hot milk into the yolk mixture and return to the heat. Cook until thickened. (Do not boil or mixture will curdle.) Stir into the melted chocolate mixture.

4. Strain the chocolate custard into the double cream and stir in the remaining rum. Chill, then transfer to an ice-cream maker and freeze as manufacturer directs. Spoon into a freezerproof container and stir in the rum-soaked raisins. Freeze until firm, but still spreadable; about 1 hour.

5. Chill a 1½ l/2½ pt ice-cream bombe mould or freezerproof glass mixing bowl. Soften the ice cream slightly. Spread on base and up side of the chilled mould. Return to the freezer.

6. Prepare the mousse: Soak the sultanas in 50 ml/2 fl oz rum for 2 hours. Bring 50 ml/2 fl oz cream to the boil. Stir in the white chocolate. Stir in the remaining rum and the rum-soaked raisins. Cool.

7. With an electric mixer, beat the egg whites until frothy. Add the cream of tartar and continue beating until stiff peaks form. Add the sugar a tablespoon at a time, beating well after each addition, until stiff and glossy. Fold into the white chocolate mixture.

8. Beat the remaining cream until soft peaks form. Fold into the mousse mixture. Spoon the white chocolate mousse into the centre of the mould. Cover tightly and freeze overnight.

9. Prepare the sauce: Process the white chocolate in a food processor to fine crumbs. Bring the cream and cinnamon to the boil and with the machine running, pour in the hot cream. Strain into a bowl and stir in the butter and rum. Cool.

10. To serve: turn out bombe and pipe a border of cream around the bottom edge and top. Soften in the refrigerator before serving with the sauce.

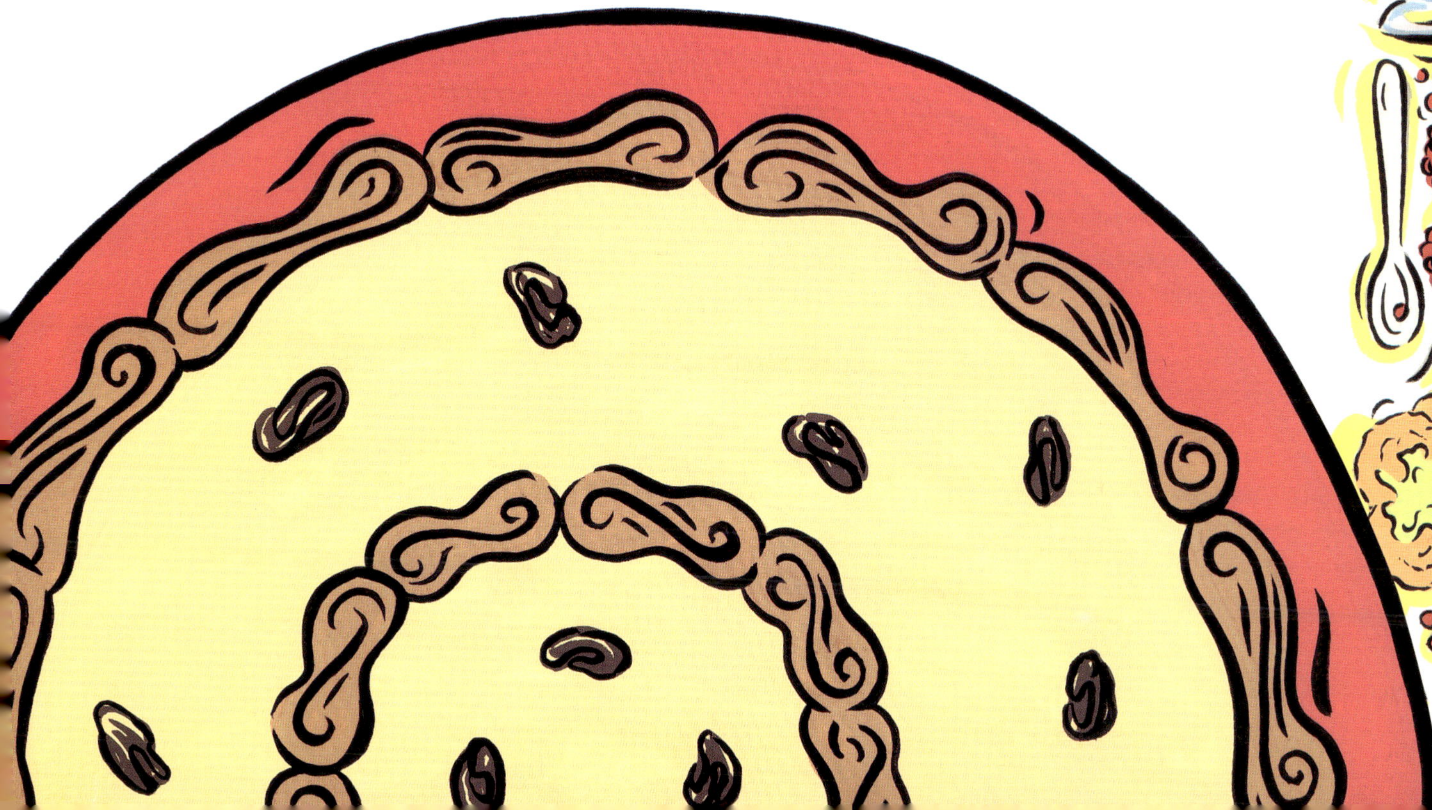

Frozen Chocolate-Coconut and Macadamia Terrine

8–10 SERVINGS

MOUSSE

225 g/8 oz good-quality white chocolate, chopped
600 ml/1 pt double cream
120 ml/4 fl oz milk
10 egg yolks
2 Tbsp granulated sugar
45 g/1½ oz desiccated coconut
120 ml/4 fl oz tinned sweetened coconut cream
2 Tbsp dark or light rum or 2 tsp rum essence
100 g/4 oz unsalted macadamia nuts

DARK CHOCOLATE GLAZE

225 g/8 oz good-quality plain or bittersweet chocolate, chopped
75 g/3 oz unsalted butter
1½ Tbsp golden syrup
175 ml/6 fl oz double cream

1. Line the bottom and sides of a 25 x 10 cm/10 x 4 inch loaf tin or terrine with cling film, smoothing out as many wrinkles as possible. Heat the white chocolate and 50 ml/2 fl oz cream until melted.

2. Bring 250 ml/8 fl oz cream and the milk to the boil. With an electric mixer, beat the egg yolks with the sugar until thickened. Whisk the hot cream-milk mixture into the yolks and return to the heat. Cook until thickened. (Do not boil or the mixture will curdle.) Remove from heat and stir in the melted white chocolate mixture, desiccated coconut, coconut cream and rum. Cool in the refrigerator.

3. Beat the remaining cream until stiff peaks just begin to form. Fold into the mixture.

4. Spoon half the mousse mixture into the terrine. Cover and freeze until firm. Refrigerate the remaining mousse mixture.

5. When the mixture in the terrine is firm, sprinkle over the nuts. Spoon in the remaining mousse and freeze overnight.

6. Heat the glaze ingredients until melted. Invert the mousse on to a wire rack and lift off terrine. Pour the glaze over the top. Freeze 3–4 hours until set.

Frozen Raspberry Mousse-Ring

8 SERVINGS

My friend Carole gave me this recipe. It is a frozen mousse with a vibrant colour and a creamy texture achieved by using a cooked meringue instead of a gelatine base.

450 g/1 lb raspberries, plus extra for serving
175 g/6 oz caster sugar
2 to 3 tsp lemon juice
2 egg whites
¼ tsp cream of tartar
2 Tbsp raspberry-flavoured liqueur
250 ml/8 fl oz double cream

Fresh mint sprigs for decoration (optional)

1. Purée the raspberries in a food processor. Press through a nonmetallic sieve into a bowl. Pour one-third of the purée into a bowl and stir in 50 g/2 oz sugar and a tablespoon of lemon juice. Add a little more sugar or lemon juice if necessary. Cover and refrigerate. Set aside remaining purée.

2. Put the egg whites, cream of tartar, 2 tablespoons lemon juice and remaining 100 g/4 oz sugar in a large heatproof bowl and set over a saucepan of just simmering water. With an electric mixer, beat until the beaters leave a trail on the bottom of the bowl. Increase the speed to high, and continue beating until the whites are stiff and glossy, 7 minutes. Remove the bowl from heat and continue beating until mixture cools, about 3 minutes. Stir the raspberry-flavoured liqueur into the remaining raspberry purée and fold into the meringue mixture.

3. Beat the cream until soft peaks form. Fold gently into the raspberry meringue mixture. Rinse a 1.4 l/2½ pt ring mould and drain but do not dry. Spoon the mousse mixture into the mould. Freeze, covered, 4–6 hours or overnight.

4. To turn out, uncover the mould and run a sharp knife around the top edge. Dip into warm water for about 5 seconds and dry the base. Invert a serving plate over the mould then, holding the plate and mould together tightly, invert both together, giving a firm shake to release the mousse. Carefully remove the mould. To serve, fill the centre of the mousse with raspberries and decorate with mint sprigs, if you like. Serve with the raspberry purée.

Pineapple-Pecan Ice-Cream

with Pecan Butterscotch Sauce

6–8 SERVINGS

This is a delicious combination of flavours, which make an unusual summertime dessert.

ICE-CREAM

225 g/8 oz chopped fresh pineapple
175 g/6 oz granulated sugar
1 large egg
3 large egg yolks
1 Tbsp cornflour
350 ml/12 fl oz milk
1 tsp vanilla essence
2 Tbsp dark rum (optional)
350 ml/12 fl oz double cream
100 g/4 oz broken pecan pieces, lightly toasted

PECAN BUTTERSCOTCH SAUCE

225 g/8 oz golden syrup
225 g/8 oz soft brown sugar, plus 2 Tbsp
100 g/4 oz butter cut into pieces
175 ml/6 fl oz double cream

1. Prepare the ice-cream: Simmer the pineapple and 50 g/2 oz sugar, stirring occasionally until sugar dissolves, about 5 minutes. Turn into a nonmetallic strainer set over a bowl and allow to drain (reserve syrup for another use).

2. With a wire whisk, beat the egg and egg yolks with the remaining sugar until lightened in colour and thickened, 3 minutes. Whisk in the cornflour.

3. Bring the milk to the boil and pour over the egg mixture, beating constantly. Return mixture to the saucepan and cook, whisking, until mixture comes back to the boil. Boil 1 minute, whisking, then strain into a large bowl. Cool, then stir in the vanilla and pineapple mixture and refrigerate 1 hour.

4. Stir in the cream and transfer to an ice-cream maker. Freeze as manufacturer directs. Spoon into a container and stir in the toasted pecans to distribute them evenly, then freeze 2–3 hours or overnight.

5. Prepare the sauce: Bring the golden syrup, brown sugar and butter to the boil until sugar has dissolved. Stir in the pecans and boil 2 minutes, remove from heat. Cool then stir in cream. Soften the ice-cream slightly. Scoop into bowls and top with the sauce.

CHAPTER FIVE

CUSTARDS, MOUSSES and SOUFFLES

Bittersweet Chocolate Mousse

6 SERVINGS

One of the world's favourite desserts – Try rum or orange-flavoured liqueur for a change.

225 g/8 oz good-quality bittersweet chocolate, chopped
4 Tbsp water
2 Tbsp unsalted butter, softened
2 Tbsp cognac
3 large eggs, separated
1/4 tsp cream of tartar
2 to 3 Tbsp caster sugar
120 ml/4 fl oz double cream

1. Put the chocolate and water into a medium saucepan and melt over low heat until smooth, stirring frequently. Remove from heat and beat in the butter and cognac. Beat the egg yolks lightly then beat into the chocolate mixture; the chocolate will thicken. Set aside.

2. Beat the egg whites until frothy. Add the cream of tartar and continue to beat until soft peaks form. Beat in the sugar a tablespoon at a time, beating well after each addition until stiff and glossy. Beat a large spoonful of whites into the chocolate mixture to lighten it and reserve the remaining whites.

3. Beat the cream until soft peaks form. Reserve half the cream for decoration. Spoon half the cream over the chocolate mixture and fold into with remaining whites. Spoon into a glass serving bowl or into individual dessert dishes. Refrigerate overnight.

4. Spoon the remaining cream into a decorating bag fitted with a medium star nozzle and refrigerate. When the mousse is set, decorate with a rosette or scroll in the centre of the bowl or on each individual dessert. Serve.

Strawberry-Mint Fools

4 SERVINGS

A fool is an old-fashioned dessert made from a fresh fruit purée swirled into whipped cream. It makes a quick and simple, but delicious dessert. Look for ripe, full-flavoured berries.

450 g/1 lb fresh ripe strawberries, hulled and quartered
3 to 4 Tbsp sugar
1 Tbsp fresh shredded mint
120 ml/4 fl oz soured cream or natural yogurt
120 ml/4 fl oz double cream

Fresh mint sprigs for decoration (optional)

1. Put the strawberries in a medium bowl and sprinkle with the sugar and the mint; the amount of sugar depends on the sweetness of the strawberries. Using a fork or potato masher, lightly crush the berries until the juices begin to run. Allow the mixture to stand about 20 minutes, stirring occasionally until all the sugar dissolves.

2. Strain the juices into a small bowl and whisk in the soured cream. Beat the cream until soft peaks form. Fold in the soured cream mixture.

3. Spoon alternate layers of crushed strawberries and cream into individual glass dessert dishes, ending with a layer of strawberries. Using a spoon or knife, gently swirl the layers in each dish, but do not mix well. Decorate with a mint sprig if you like.

TIP: Do not assemble too far in advance, or the cream and strawberries may become too liquid.

Individual Sticky Toffee Puddings

4 SERVINGS

This typical British pudding is like a tiny moist sponge cake with a caramel-toffee sauce, cooked together.

CUSTARD SAUCE
(crème anglaise p.45)

CARAMEL-TOFFEE SAUCE
Melted butter for greasing
75 g/2½ oz granulated sugar
2 Tbsp water
50 ml/2 fl oz double cream, heated

PUDDING
100 g/4 oz unsalted butter, softened
100 g/4 oz soft brown sugar
4 eggs, separated
100 g/4 oz self-raising flour or 100 g/4 oz plain flour plus 1 tsp baking powder, sifted
50 g/2 oz chopped dates
Butter for greasing

1. Prepare the crème anglaise (p.45), but delete the lemon rind and use the pod and tiny seeds of one vanilla pod. Stir in 1 tablespoon cornflour into the beaten egg yolks and the sugar before whisking in the milk.

2. Prepare the caramel-toffee sauce: Butter four 300 ml/½ pt ramekins. Put the sugar in a saucepan and drizzle over the water to moisten. Cook over low heat until sugar dissolves. Boil until a golden caramel forms. Remove from heat and standing well back, add the warm cream. Return to the heat and stir until melted and smooth.

3. Prepare the pudding: Preheat oven to 180°C/ 350°F/Gas Mark 4. Beat the butter and sugar until fluffy and lightened in colour, 2 minutes. Beat in the egg yolks one at a time, beating well after each addition. Fold all but 2 to 3 tablespoons of the flour mixture into the butter-egg yolk mixture.

4. Beat the egg whites until soft peaks form. Stir a spoonful of whites into the mixture to lighten it, then fold in the remaining whites. Toss the dates in the reserved 2 to 3 tablespoons of the flour mixture and sprinkle over the batter, then gently fold in. Divide equally between the ramekins.

5. Cover each ramekin with greased baking paper. Secure ramekin; cover with foil. Put ramekins in a roasting tin and pour in enough boiling water to come halfway up sides. Bake 40 minutes. Turn out and spoon over sauce. Serve with the custard.

Iced Lemon Soufflé
with Caramel Syrup

6–8 SERVINGS

CARAMEL SYRUP
350 g/12 oz sugar
50 ml/2 fl oz cold water
175 ml/6 fl oz hot water

LEMON SOUFFLE
120 ml/4 fl oz plus 2 Tbsp water
Grated rind and juice of 2 lemons
300 g/10 oz granulated sugar
4 eggs, separated
2 Tbsp cold water
1 Tbsp unflavoured gelatine
¼ tsp cream of tartar
300 ml/½ pt double cream

120 ml/4 fl oz double cream, whipped

1. Prepare the caramel syrup: Put the sugar in a saucepan and drizzle over the cold water to moisten. Heat until the sugar dissolves. Boil until syrup turns a deep caramel colour, 10 minutes, without stirring. Remove from heat and, standing well back, add the hot water to the caramel; take care – the mixture will splatter. Return to the heat and stir until melted and smooth. Pour into a bowl and refrigerate.

2. Cut a piece of foil or greaseproof paper long enough to encircle a soufflé dish allowing a 5 cm/2 inch overlap. Fold in half lengthways and wrap around the dish so the collar extends about 7.5 cm/3 inches above the top. Secure with string. Lightly oil the inside of the collar.

3. Prepare the lemon soufflé: Put the 120 ml/4 fl oz water, lemon rind and juice and sugar in a medium saucepan and boil for 5 minutes.

4. Process the egg yolks in a food processor for 30 seconds. With the machine running, slowly pour the boiling syrup on to the yolks and process 1 minute until creamy and pale.

5. Put 2 tablespoons of water in a small bowl and sprinkle over the gelatine. Allow to stand 2–3 minutes, then put into a small bowl and set over a saucepan of simmering water, stirring to dissolve. Add the gelatine to the egg mixture and process 5 seconds until blended. Pour into a large mixing bowl and refrigerate until mixture begins to set.

6. Beat the whites until frothy. Add the cream of tartar and beat on high speed until soft peaks form. Beat the cream until soft peaks form. Fold the cream into the chilled, setting-yolk mixture, then fold in the whites. Pour the mixture into the prepared dish. Refrigerate overnight.

7. Remove the string and peel the paper from the soufflé. Pipe rosettes or scrolls of whipped cream decoratively around the top edge. Serve immediately with the chilled caramel syrup.

Crème Brûlée
with Strawberries

6 SERVINGS

Crème brûlée is an international favourite. The addition of small or alpine strawberries makes it even more special. Try other berries and fruits if you like.

25 g/1 oz unsalted butter, softened
50 g/2 oz good quality strawberry jam
36 small or alpine strawberries
900 ml/1½ pt double cream
1 vanilla pod, split lengthways
6 egg yolks
120 ml/4 fl oz caster sugar
2 Tbsp orange-flavoured liqueur or brandy
75 g/3 oz soft brown sugar

1. Lightly butter six 120 ml/4 fl oz ramekins. Stir the strawberry jam to loosen it, then divide it equally between the ramekins, spreading it even only on the bottoms. Put six strawberries in each ramekin and set them in a large roasting tin or ovenproof dish; then set aside.

2. Preheat oven to 160°C/300°F/Gas Mark 2. Put the cream in a medium saucepan. With a small sharp knife, scrape the tiny black seeds from the vanilla pod and add to the cream. Bring to the boil over medium-high heat, stirring frequently. Remove from heat, cover and allow to stand for about 15 minutes.

3. Beat the egg yolks and sugar in a large bowl until foamy and lightened in colour, 2–3 minutes. Bring the cream back to the boil and whisk into the egg yolk mixture until well blended. Strain into a large measuring cup or jug, then divide the mixture equally among the prepared ramekins.

4. Pour enough boiling water into the roasting tin to come halfway up the sides of the ramekins. Cover the tin with foil and bake 25 minutes until the custards are just set (the centres should still be soft – do not overcook). Remove to a wire rack to cool completely then refrigerate overnight.

5. Preheat the grill. Sprinkle an even layer of brown sugar over the surface of each custard and set them on a baking sheet. Grill 30–60 seconds until the sugar melts and caramelizes, rotating the baking sheet for even melting. (Do not allow the sugar to burn or the custard will curdle.) Refrigerate the crème brûlée immediately to stop cooking and allow the caramel to harden. Chill before serving.

Crème Caramel

6 SERVINGS

This is one of my all-time favourite recipes – the silky custard and slightly bitter caramel combine to make a classic dessert.

450 g/1 lb sugar
50 ml/2 fl oz water
500 ml/18 fl oz milk
175 ml/6 fl oz double cream
1 vanilla pod, split lengthways
4 large eggs
4 large yolks

1. Put 225 g/8 oz of the sugar in a heavy-based medium saucepan and drizzle over the water to moisten it. Set over medium-low heat until the sugar dissolves. Boil, without stirring, until the syrup turns a deep caramel; this will take about 6 minutes.

2. Immediately pour the hot caramel into a 1.4 l/2½ pt soufflé dish or other heatproof mould and carefully swirl the dish to coat the bottom and sides evenly. Set aside to cool.

3. Preheat oven to 170°C/325°F/Gas Mark 3. Put the milk and cream into a saucepan. Scrape the tiny black seeds from the vanilla pod and add to the milk and cream. Bring to the boil.

4. Whisk the eggs and egg yolks with the remaining sugar until foamy and lightened in colour. Pour the boiling milk-mixture on to the egg mixture, whisking constantly. Carefully strain the custard into the caramel-lined dish and cover with foil.

5. Fold a clean dishcloth and use to form a base in a large roasting tin or dish. Set the soufflé dish or mould on to the towel and pour in enough boiling water to come halfway up the side. Bake 40–45 minutes or until just set. Carefully remove to a wire rack to cool about 30 minutes. Refrigerate 6–8 hours or overnight.

6. To turn out, carefully run a sharp knife around the edge of the dish to loosen the custard. Cover the dish with a serving plate and, holding them tightly, invert the dish and plate together. Gently lift one side of the soufflé dish or mould, allowing the caramel to run over the side, then lift off the dish. Cut in wedges and serve with a little caramel.

Floating Island with Blackcurrant Coulis

6 SERVINGS

Floating island gets its name from the moulded meringue sitting in a pool of custard sauce or crème anglaise. This version uses a blackcurrant coulis to glaze the meringue island instead of the traditional caramel.
Use any other favourite berry if blackcurrants are unavailable.

BLACKCURRANT COULIS

450 g/1 lb fresh blackcurrants, stalks removed, rinsed and drained, or frozen blackcurrants (thawed)
50 ml/2 fl oz water
50 g/2 oz sugar
2 Tbsp lemon juice

MERINGUE

4 egg whites
1/4 tsp cream of tartar
100 g/4 oz caster sugar
1 tsp vanilla essence
Crème Anglaise (p.45)

Chopped hazelnuts or pistachios for decoration

1. Process the blackcurrants, water, sugar and lemon juice in a food processor. Press through a non-metallic strainer into a bowl. Refrigerate.

2. Prepare the crème anglaise as for lemon crème anglaise (p.45), but delete the lemon rind and add one vanilla pod with its seeds to the milk or flavour with 2 teaspoons vanilla essence.

3. Prepare the meringue. Preheat oven to 180°C/350°F/Gas Mark 4. Lightly butter a 900 ml/1 1/2 pt charlotte mould or soufflé dish. Beat the egg whites until frothy. Add the cream of tartar and continue beating until stiff peaks form. Add the sugar 2 tablespoons at a time, beating well after each addition, folding in the last 2 tablespoons of sugar with the vanilla. Spoon into the mould.

4. Set the mould or dish into a deep roasting tin and pour in enough boiling water to come at least 2.5 cm/1 inch up the sides. Bake about 25 minutes until the top is golden and springy to the touch. Cool and then refrigerate overnight.

5. Turn out on to a large shallow serving dish. Ladle the crème anglaise around the meringue island and spoon the blackcurrant coulis over the top of the meringue. Sprinkle the top with the hazelnuts or pistachios and serve.

Creamy Rice Pudding
with Tropical Fruits

8–10 SERVINGS

750 ml/28 fl oz milk
250 ml/8 fl oz double cream
150 g/5 oz short-grain rice
1 vanilla pod, split lengthways
2 to 4 Tbsp sugar
2 Tbsp sultanas
2 eggs
1/2 tsp cinnamon
1/4 tsp allspice

450 g/1 lb chopped chopped fruits, such as mango, kiwi, papaya, melon, grapes, peeled lychees and strawberries
3 Tbsp brown sugar for sprinkling

Fresh mint sprigs for decoration

1. Put the milk, cream, rice, split vanilla pod, sugar and sultanas into a large heavy-based saucepan or casserole. Bring to the boil over medium heat, then reduce the heat to low and simmer about 20 minutes, stirring frequently.

2. Whisk the eggs in a small bowl and pour in a little of the milky rice mixture, beating well. Slowly pour the egg mixture back into the rice mixture, stirring constantly. Cook over low heat until the mixture thickens, about 1 minute. (Do not boil or the eggs will curdle.) Remove from heat and stir in the cinnamon and allspice and pour into a large bowl. Cool slightly, stirring occasionally to prevent a skin from forming.

3. Spoon the warm pudding into a shallow serving bowl and arrange the fruit over the top. Sprinkle the brown sugar over the fruit, decorate with the fresh mint sprigs and serve while still warm. Alternatively, refrigerate the pudding and serve cold with the fruit.

Cherry-Cheese Blintzes
with Cherry Cognac Sauce

ABOUT 12 BLINTZES

Blintzes are a Jewish-American treat made by filling thin crêpes with a sweetened soft-cheese mixture, then folding and frying them. They are delicious with this cherry cognac sauce.

FOR THE CREPES

75 g/3 oz plain flour, sifted
1/2 tsp salt
2 Tbsp caster sugar
2 eggs, lightly beaten
250 ml/8 fl oz milk
50 ml/2 fl oz water
2 Tbsp cognac (optional)
25 g/1 oz unsalted butter, melted, plus extra for frying

DRIED CHERRY-CHEESE FILLING

50 g/2 oz dried sour cherries
50 ml/2 fl oz hot water
225 g/8 oz cottage cheese or ricotta cheese
1 (75 g/3 oz) carton cream cheese, softened
3 to 4 Tbsp granulated sugar
1/2 tsp vanilla essence

CHERRY COGNAC SAUCE

450 g/1 lb sweet cherries, stoned
120 ml/4 fl oz cognac
100 g/4 oz granulated sugar
2 tsp cornflour dissolved in 1 1/2 Tbsp cold water

2 to 4 Tbsp butter for frying

1. Prepare the crêpes: Sift the flour, salt and sugar into a bowl and make a well in the centre. Pour in the beaten egg and whisk in the eggs and then the milk and water until a smooth batter forms. Stir in the cognac, if using and strain into a large measuring jug. Allow to stand about 30 minutes.

2. Heat a small nonstick crêpe pan. Stir the melted butter into the crêpe batter and brush the hot pan with a little of the extra melted butter. Pour in 2–3 tablespoons of batter and rotate the pan covering the bottom with a thin layer of batter. Cook until the top is set and the bottom is golden brown, about 1 minute. Turn and cook the other side for 30 seconds until set. Slide on to a plate. Cook the remaining crêpes in the same way.

3. Prepare the cheese mixture: Soak the dried cherries in the hot water for about 20 minutes. In a large bowl beat the cottage cheese or ricotta cheese, cream cheese, sugar and vanilla until smooth; stir in the dried cherries.

4. Spread a little of the cheese mixture along the centre of each crêpe and roll up.

5. Prepare the sauce: Bring the cherries, cognac and sugar to the boil in a saucepan. Stir the cornflour mixture, then stir into the cherry liquid and boil until thick, about 1 minute.

6. Heat 2 to 3 tablespoons butter in a large frying pan. Add the blintzes in batches if necessary, and cook until golden on both sides, about 3 minutes. Serve immediately with the hot sauce.

Chocolate Tiramisù

10–12 SERVINGS

Tiramisù translates as "pick-me-up". This classic Italian dessert will do more than pick you up, it will transport you to heaven.

1 (495 g/17½ oz) carton mascarpone* cheese, at room temperature
50 g/2 oz icing sugar, sifted
350 ml/12 fl oz freshly brewed espresso or strong coffee, chilled
600 ml/1 pt double cream
175 g/6 oz good-quality plain or bittersweet chocolate, melted and cooled
6 Tbsp coffee-flavoured liqueur
50 g/2 oz plain or bittersweet chocolate, grated
2 Tbsp chocolate-flavoured liqueur
1 (200 g/7 oz) packet savoiardi** biscuits (Italian ladies' fingers)
Cocoa powder for dusting, sifted

1. Put the mascarpone and sugar in a large bowl and beat until smooth and creamy, about 1 minute. Gradually beat in about 50 ml/2 fl oz espresso or strong coffee; do not overbeat.

2. Beat the cream until soft peaks form. Gently fold the cream into the mascarpone mixture, then spoon half the mixture back into the cream bowl. Fold the melted chocolate and 2 tablespoons of the coffee-flavoured liqueur into half the mascarpone-cream mixture and set aside. Fold the grated chocolate and the chocolate-flavoured liqueur into the remaining mascarpone cream mixture; set aside.

3. Put half the remaining espresso or strong coffee and 2 tablespoons coffee-flavoured liqueur in a shallow dish. Dip one side of a savoiardi biscuit into the coffee mixture and plate it dry-side down in a 32.5 x 22 cm/13 x 9 inch baking dish. Continue with half the biscuits to form a lightly packed layer. Drizzle over any remaining espresso or coffee mixture. Spoon the chocolate-mascarpone mixture over the biscuit layer in the dish, smoothing the surface evenly.

4. Pour the remaining coffee and liqueur into the dish. Dip the remaining biscuits into the espresso mixture, layering them over the chocolate mascarpone mixture. Drizzle over any remaining espresso or coffee mixture. Spoon the remaining grated chocolate-mascarpone mixture over the second layer of biscuits and smooth the top, leaving no spaces between the filling and sides of the dish. Cover the dish with cling film and refrigerate overnight. To serve, dust with a thick layer of cocoa.

*Mascarpone is a smooth, sweet Italian cream cheese, available in large supermarkets and gourmet shops.

**Savoiardi biscuits are Italian/French ladies' fingers, with a crisp finish.

Chocolate Pavlova with Exotic Fruits and White Chocolate Cream

6–8 SERVINGS

Both Australia and New Zealand claim to have invented this delicate meringue-based dessert to honor the famous ballerina, Anna Pavlova. This is a chocolate version.

MERINGUE

4 egg whites, at room temperature
¼ tsp cream of tartar
225 g/8 oz caster sugar
3 Tbsp cocoa powder, sifted
1 tsp cornflour
1 tsp cider vinegar

WHITE CHOCOLATE CREAM

100 g/4 oz good-quality white chocolate, chopped
120 ml/4 fl oz single cream
15 g/½ oz unsalted butter
1 tsp vanilla essence
250 ml/8 fl oz double cream
550 g/1¼ lb sliced mixed exotic fruits such as kiwi, mango, papaya or 550 g/1¼ lb mixed strawberries, raspberries and blueberries

Fresh mint sprigs for decoration

1. Preheat oven to 170˚C/325˚F/Gas Mark 3. Place a sheet of nonstick baking paper on a large baking sheet and draw a 20 cm/8 inch circle.

2. With an electric mixer, beat the egg whites until frothy. Add the cream of tartar and continue beating until stiff peaks form. Sprinkle in the sugar, 2 tablespoons at a time, making sure each addition is well blended before adding the next, until whites are stiff and glossy. Fold in the sifted cocoa and cornflour mixture then fold in the vinegar.

3. Spoon the meringue mixture on to the centre of the circle marked on the paper. Using the back of a metal spoon spread evenly, building up the sides higher than the centre. Bake in the centre of the oven until set, 45–50 minutes. Turn off the oven and leave to stand in the oven 45 minutes longer; the meringue may crack or sink, but it does not matter. Cool the meringue completely and carefully transfer to a serving plate.

4. Heat the white chocolate and single cream until smooth. Beat in the butter and vanilla and cool.

5. Beat the cream until soft peaks form. Stir half the cream into the chocolate mixture, then fold in the remaining cream and spoon into the centre of the meringue. Arrange the fruits over the white chocolate cream and decorate with the mint.

Chocolate Mint Crisps

MAKES ABOUT 24 MINTS

These easy-to-make after-dinner mints are perfect with coffee. As an alternative, use orange essence instead of mint.

Vegetable oil for greasing
4 Tbsp granulated sugar
50 ml/2 fl oz water
1 tsp peppermint essence
225 g/8 oz plain or bittersweet chocolate, chopped

1. Using a pastry brush, brush a biscuit sheet with vegetable oil and set aside.

2. Put the sugar in a saucepan with the water and bring to the boil over medium heat, swirling pan until sugar dissolves. Boil rapidly until the sugar reaches 140°C/280°F on a sugar thermometer. Remove from heat and swirl in the peppermint essence. Pour on to the greased biscuit sheet and allow to cool completely. Do not touch, as sugar syrup is hot and can cause serious burns.

3. When cold and hard, lift off the biscuit sheet and break into small pieces. Put the pieces into the bowl of a food processor fitted with a metal blade and process until fine crumbs form; do not overprocess.

4. Line two biscuit sheets with nonstick baking paper or foil. Put the chocolate in a small bowl and set over a saucepan of just simmering water. Stir frequently until melted and smooth. Remove from heat and stir in the ground sugar-mint mixture.

5. Using a teaspoon, drop small mounds of the mixture on to the biscuit sheets. Using the back of a spoon, spread into 35 cm/1½ inch circles. Cool, then refrigerate until set, at least 1 hour. Peel the mints off the paper and refrigerate in an airtight container.

***TIP:** If you do not have a sugar thermometer, test the temperature of the boiling sugar by pouring a few drops of syrup into a small bowl of cold water; it should become brittle and snap easily within 1 minute. Do not touch the sugar until it cools in the water for a few seconds.*

Chocolate Truffles

ABOUT 24 TRUFFLES

Most truffles are made from a ganache base – a mixture of chocolate and cream or butter with the addition of a flavouring such as cognac or another liqueur. Truffles can be rolled in cocoa or finely chopped nuts, or dipped in chocolate.

250 ml/8 fl oz double cream
300 g/10 oz good-quality bittersweet chocolate, chopped
25 g/1 oz unsalted butter
2 Tbsp brandy or other favourite liqueur

Cocoa powder for dusting, sifted
450 g/1 lb bittersweet chocolate

1. Bring the cream to the boil. Remove from heat all of the chocolate, stirring until melted and smooth. Beat in the butter until melted and stir in the liqueur. Strain into a bowl and cool to room temperature. Refrigerate until thickened and firm, about 1 hour.

2. Line a biscuit sheet with foil or nonstick baking paper. With a teaspoon, form mixture into small balls and place on the prepared biscuit sheet.

3. If dusting with cocoa, sift about 50 g/2 oz cocoa into a small bowl. Drop each ball into the cocoa and toss with a fork to coat on all sides, then roll lightly between the palms of your hands, rounding the balls. (Dust your hands with a little cocoa to prevent the truffles from sticking.) Do not worry if the truffles are not perfectly round as an irregular shape is more authentic.

4. Shake cocoa-coated truffles in a dry sieve to remove any excess cocoa. Refrigerate covered in an airtight container for up to 2 weeks, or freeze for up to 2 months. Soften slightly at room temperature before serving.

5. If coating with melted chocolate, do not roll in cocoa, but freeze for 1 hour after forming into balls. Melt the chocolate in a small bowl and, using a fork, dip balls into melted chocolate one at a time, tapping fork on side of bowl to shake off excess. Place on the prepared baking sheet and refrigerate immediately to keep coating shiny. (If melted chocolate thickens, reheat gently to thin.)

Almond Tile Biscuits

15 BISCUITS

These popular French biscuits – tuiles aux amandes – are so called because they resemble the curved roof tiles seen all over France. Although they are not difficult to make, they do require a little patience and practice in the beginning.

50 g/2 oz whole blanched almonds, lightly toasted
100 g/4 oz caster sugar
45 g/1½ oz unsalted butter, softened
2 egg whites
½ tsp almond essence
25 g/1 oz extra fine flour, sifted
75 g/3 oz slivered almonds

1. Process the blanched almonds and 2 tablespoons of the sugar in a food processor until fine crumbs form. Pour into a small bowl and set aside.

2. Preheat oven to 200°C/ 400°F/Gas Mark 6. Generously butter two or more biscuit sheets. With an electric mixer, beat the butter until creamy, about 1 minute. Add the remaining sugar and beat until light and fluffy. Gradually beat in the egg whites and almond essence until well blended. Resift the already sifted flour and fold into the butter mixture, then fold in the reserved almond-sugar mixture.

3. Begin by working in batches of four biscuits on each sheet. Drop tablespoons of batter about 15 cm/ 6 inches apart on to the biscuit sheet. With the back of a moistened spoon, spread each mound of batter into very thin 7.5 cm/3 inch rounds. Each round should be transparent; it does not matter if you make a few holes, the batter will spread evenly and fill them in. Sprinkle tops with some slivered almonds.

4. Bake one sheet at a time, for about 5 minutes. Remove biscuit sheet to wire rack and, working quickly, use a thin-bladed metal spatula to loosen the edge of a hot biscuit. Transfer to a rolling pin or glass tumbler and gently press sides down to shape each biscuit. Repeat with the remaining biscuit rounds.

5. If biscuits become too firm to transfer, return the biscuit sheet to the oven for 30 seconds to soften, then proceed as above. Continue baking and shaping with the remaining dough. When cool transfer immediately to airtight containers in single layers. These biscuits are fragile.

TIP: *If biscuits become limp, reshape by placing them on an ungreased baking sheet and baking again at 40°C/100°F until completely flattened, 2–3 minutes. Reshape over rolling pin as instructed above.*

Cream-Filled Brandy Snaps

ABOUT 24–30

These lacy cognac-scented snaps are filled with a cognac-flavoured whipped cream. They make an elegant after-dinner treat.

BRANDY SNAPS

Butter for greasing
100 g/4 oz unsalted butter, cut into pieces
3 Tbsp golden syrup
50 g/2 oz granulated sugar
75 g/3 oz soft brown sugar
1 tsp ground ginger
2 Tbsp cognac
50 g/2 oz plain flour, sifted

COGNAC CREAM

300 ml/½ pt double cream
1 Tbsp granulated sugar
½ tsp vanilla essence
2 Tbsp cognac

1. Preheat oven to 180°C/350°F/Gas Mark 4. Butter two or more baking sheets; or use nonstick baking sheets. Lightly oil the handles of two wooden spoons. Put the butter, golden syrup, sugars and ginger in a saucepan and bring to the boil over medium heat, stirring until sugars dissolve. Remove from heat, stir in the cognac and the flour until well blended and smooth. Place the saucepan in a shallow bowl of hot water (this will keep the batter from hardening).

2. Working in batches of four biscuits on each 15 cm/6 inches apart on the sheets. Using the back of a moistened spoon, spread each mound into 7.5 cm/3 inch rounds (the rounds will spread out even more). Bake until golden and bubbling, about 10 minutes, turning the baking sheet if the brandy snaps colour unevenly.

3. Remove the baking sheet to a wire rack to cool, about 1 minute. Working quickly, use a thin-bladed metal spatula to loosen the edge of a hot brandy snap and lift it off. Roll each biscuit around the oiled handle of a wooden spoon. Slide off the handle and transfer to a wire rack to cool completely.

4. Up to 2 hours before serving, with an electric mixer, beat the cream, sugar, vanilla and brandy until stiff peaks form. Spoon cream into a decorating bag fitted with a medium star nozzle. Pipe cream into both ends of each biscuit and place on a baking sheet. Refrigerate until ready to serve.

After-Dinner Chocolate Cream Liqueur

Surprise your guests with this homemade chocolate cream liqueur. For a real show-stopper, serve with a chocolate truffle in the middle and a tiny spoon.

1 Tbsp instant espresso or coffee powder
25 g/1 oz cocoa powder, sifted
250 ml/8 fl oz milk
250 ml/8 fl oz double cream
1 (400 g/14 oz) tin sweetened condensed milk
1 egg yolk
250 ml/8 fl oz Scotch whisky
85 ml/3 fl oz light rum
1 Tbsp vanilla essence
1 Tbsp coconut essence

1. Stir together the espresso or coffee powder and cocoa powder in a large saucepan. Gradually whisk in the milk then the cream and sweetened condensed milk and bring to the boil over medium heat, stirring frequently until well blended.

2. Beat the egg yolk in a small bowl until foamy. Pour half the hot-milk mixture over the yolk, whisking constantly, then stir the cream-egg mixture back into the saucepan. Cook over medium-low heat until the mixture thickens slightly and coats the back of a wooden spoon, about 3 minutes. Remove from heat and stir in the whisky, rum and vanilla and coconut essences. Strain into a bowl and cool, stirring constantly. Refrigerate until completely chilled, about 3–4 hours.

3. Transfer to a bottle or jar with a tight-fitting lid and store in the refrigerator for up to 1 week. Stir or shake well before serving.

Double Chocolate-Dipped Fruit

ABOUT 12 PIECES

About 12 pieces of fruit such as strawberries, cherries, Cape gooseberries, orange segments, kiwi fruit, pitted prunes, pitted dates, dried apricots, dried pears
175 g/6 oz good-quality white chocolate, chopped
75 g/3 oz good-quality plain or bittersweet chocolate, chopped

1. Clean and prepare the fruits. Wipe strawberries with a soft cloth or brush gently with a pastry brush; wash firm fruits like cherries or grapes, dry well and set on kitchen paper to absorb any remaining moisture. Peel or cut any other fruits being used and choose the plumpest dried fruits. Line a baking sheet with nonstick baking paper or foil.

2. Put the white chocolate in a small heatproof bowl and set over a saucepan of hot water. Stir frequently until melted and smooth. Remove from heat and then cool slightly.

3. Holding fruits by the stem or end and at an angle, dip about two-thirds of the fruit into the chocolate. Allow excess to drip off and place on the prepared baking sheet. Continue dipping all the fruits; if the chocolate becomes too thick, heat gently over the hot water to thin. Refrigerate until set, about 30 minutes.

4. Put the plain chocolate into another small heatproof bowl and set over a saucepan of hot water. Stir frequently until melted and smooth. Remove from heat and cool slightly.

5. Lift the half-coated fruits from the baking sheet and, holding each piece by the stem or end, and at the opposite angle, dip bottom third of each piece into the chocolate, creating a chevron effect. Set on the lined baking sheet and refrigerate until set. Soften slightly at room temperature before serving.

Index